I'M FINE

I'M FINE

A Story of Overcoming Adversity Through God's Grace

Rick Toomey, Ed.D.

Copyright © 2014 Rick Toomey

4027 Lakeland Drive

Kingsport, TN, 37664

ortoomey@gmail.com

I'm fine: a story of overcoming adversity through
God's grace

Trade paper edition

ISBN: 978-0-9916245-0-8

Publisher Cataloging-in-Publication

Library of Congress Control Number: 2014907153

Printed In the United States of America

First Printing, May, 2014

Scripture taken from the Holy Bible:
American Standard Version

DEDICATION

In March of 2012, my mother, Lockey Lou Toomey, and I visited my cousin, Debra Sue McDonald, or Debbie as we call her. This book is about Debbie's life. I am writing this book for two reasons. First and foremost, I'm writing this book because a book about the life of Debbie McDonald needs to be written. Her life is extraordinary and my hope is that knowing the story of her life can inspire others the way it has inspired those who have been blessed to know Debbie.

The second reason is that as Mom and I drove home from that visit, I shared my deep felt belief that Debbie's story needed to be told and shared with a broad audience. Those who know Debbie's story are basically her family, the staff and residents of care-giving facilities where she has lived.

Mom agreed with me. I then promised I would try to tell Debbie's story through a book. Mom loved that idea and encouraged me to start it as soon as possible. I began to gather information from Mom. I sent an email to family members requesting their memories of and thoughts about Debbie.

A month after our visit, Mom, who was 91 at the time, had her second heart attack in two years and had a second stent inserted into one of her arteries. It was obvious after a few weeks that Mom would not recover from the heart attack and surgery.

Her condition began to decline rather rapidly, and on August 22, about two months after her 92nd birthday, Mom passed away in our home with my sister, my wife, and me present. Those last few months were so sweet and ones I will treasure the rest of my life.

Needless to say most things went on the back burner after Mom's death. Even though her last days were sweet and peaceful, and even though I was confident about her future being even more wonderful than her past, and even though I had many fond memories to treasure, losing one of the most important people in my life was tough. Mom shaped me more than any other human being. She had been a constant source of undying support and encouragement in my life. Those days after her death were not easy, and it was difficult to focus on other things.

About nine months later, the commitment I made to Mom began to dominate my thoughts. It really hit me when I was talking with my uncle Clint, and I shared with him that my sister, wife, and I would like to visit him. Clint said that would be great. He wanted to talk with me about what he wanted done for his funeral. I responded with, "You aren't planning on leaving us anytime soon." He laughed and said that none of the males in his family had lived past 83, and he would be 83 in three years. I realized that none of my mother's siblings might be around in a few years.

I told my wife, Marcie, after this conversation, that I needed to really focus on completing the book and set some other things aside. She agreed completely. I also joked with Marcie that I was afraid if I didn't get to work on the book Mom would find some ingenious way to discipline me for not keeping that commitment. My mother had never laid a hand on me nor raised her voice with me, but she was the master disciplinarian.

For example, when I was a seven-year old I couldn't swim, and as a result, was not supposed to be on the creek behind our house. Well, my cousin, Jerry, and I had found an old wooden handmade boat lodged on a log behind our house and for a few days we would get in the boat and play on our way home from school. Then one day it began to sink with me in it. I jumped to the edge of the bank safely but in the process got my jeans pretty wet and muddy. I knew immediately I was in big trouble. Even though I changed clothes and hid my jeans under the bed hoping they would magically clean themselves, I still knew there was a reckoning in my future. Needless to say Mom found them and discovered how I had broken the rule and was on and in the creek. Mom asked me what discipline I deserved. I went straight for a spanking because it was quick and not that painful. Mom proceeded to tell me that she was afraid I would not really learn a lesson from a spanking, so she told me my discipline would be walking home from school for the next two weeks with my sister, Betty, who was four years older than me. That meant I would be walking home with about five or six older girls and listening to them do that girl talk thing for what seemed like an eternity while my friends would be playing chase, throwing ball, and having fun.

So wanting to avoid the possible "discipline" from my Mom is part of the reason for writing this. More importantly, I want to share what I know about the wonderful life of Debbie.

I'm dedicating this book to my mother because of the inspiration she was to me and others, and also because she is a significant character in the story. Even though Debbie had an incredible mother, Mom was like a second mother to her. With the early challenges Debbie faced in her life, the care of two mothers was probably needed, and my mother certainly provided the same love, devotion, nurturing, and helping hand to Debbie that she provided for my two sisters and me.

So Mom, because I believe you are looking down from above, and I know you are with us in spirit, I want you to know this book is dedicated to you. I want to remind you of the conversation I had with you a week before your death when you had a dream that God had his arms outstretched and you did not know what to do. I told you then that the next time you saw God with His arms outstretched you should run into them. I told you to do this because your work here was done. I then told you that all the people you loved, including Debbie, were doing great and that you would always be a positive and constructive part of our lives.

Thank you Mom.

Preface

My playing field is the classroom and a conversation with another person. While teaching, counseling, or consulting through the years, some people have encouraged me to write a book. I've even given thought to the books I would like to write. These books would focus on psychological and spiritual themes.

This book is not one about an issue or a concept. It is ultimately a very personal story about an exceptional woman who has demonstrated a level of courage and determination that is difficult to comprehend. I will try to explore the influences that have enabled her to gain victory over tremendous adversity.

This remarkable woman is one of my cousins, Debbie McDonald. This book is written to bring attention to her incredible life and her Lord and Savior Jesus Christ to whom she gives primary credit for everything good in her life.

The other major influences in Debbie's life have been her mom, her dad, her aunt Lockey, who was my mother, and the rest of her family. Debbie and her father, Mac, are still living. Debbie's mother, Loraine, died in 2011.

In telling Debbie's story, I want to acknowledge the influence of the rest of her family, a few dear friends, and two care-giving facilities. Those positive contributions will be described.

ACKNOWLEDGMENTS

This book would not have been written without the encouragement of my wife, Marcie, my sister, Carolyn, and other family members. Debbie's immediate family and her nurse during the hospital stay after the accident provided important input for the book.

Thanks to some dear friends, Zellie Earnest, Raj Mehta, and Greg Depriest, who took time to read the first draft and provide valuable suggestions.

I want to thank Jim Welch for graciously allowing me to quote from a wonderful article he wrote for the Kingsport Times-News. In addition, the Daily Post-Athenian and Cleveland Daily Banner were so kind to allow me to quote from articles about the McDonald family.

Finally special thanks to Susan Doran for helping with formatting the text and Lynda Snook for helping with the editing. A very special thanks to Jill and Jamie McAmis, my step-son and his wife, for developing the cover for the book. Jill chose the picture of Debbie for the front cover. This picture was taken a few months before the automobile accident in which she incurred her serious injuries. They are gifted in creative arts and graphic design and have a business in that area. They can be reached at jill@311graphics.com.

Table of Contents

RICK TOOMEY

Chapter 1

Introduction:

An Extraordinary Life

"I'm fine." This is the response any person will receive when greeting Debbie with "How are you doing?" Not occasionally, but every time. This is not only when she is doing well, but when she is hurting, feeling bad, sad, or experiencing any difficulty. Debbie's "I'm fine" is also said with conviction and with a smile. It is not said casually or out of habit. Debbie's "I'm fine" is not just a repetitive response given without reflection. This response comes from the depth of her being and makes one believe that she is really doing just fine. Why? Debbie is able to give this response because she has developed a belief system and faith that enables her to be fine regardless of the circumstances.

Why is this so remarkable? This book will attempt to describe the life of someone, who has a legitimate excuse for answering "how are you doing?" with responses like "Terrible!" "Life isn't fair," Why me?" or "Life just sucks today." But Debbie never responds that way, and I mean never.

My life has given me the opportunity to study people who have dealt with significant challenges. Throughout my career, I have worked with and observed people who are very successful and who have dealt with problems and adversity in ways that inspired or even amazed me.

However, there are very few of those that I would call truly extraordinary. When we think about people who are exceptional, we often go to those who have special talents and abilities. Usain Bolt is considered the greatest sprinter of all time. Michael Jordan is considered the greatest basketball player to ever play the game. Albert Einstein is considered to be one of the world's most brilliant minds. Although each of these people had to have the discipline to develop his natural abilities, much of their greatness had to do with the innate talents with which they were born.

This book is an exploration of greatness of another kind. The type of greatness I see in Debbie is the type that can be achieved by anyone but is, in reality, achieved by very few. This greatness is not determined by innate talents or abilities. It rather grows out of our character and the choices we make in life and the behavior we exhibit everyday and particularly in challenging times. Exceptional people, like Debbie, demonstrate strength, courage, and wisdom in the midst of tremendous adversity, whether it is of their choosing or not.

One person that comes to mind immediately is Mother Teresa. Here is a meek nun who doesn't seem to have outstanding natural talents or abilities. However, she was truly exceptional in the way she demonstrated true love to the outcasts of the world. Martin Luther King challenged us to respect people based not on the color of their skin but the content of their character in an incredible way and helped to transform our country. The way Helen Keller overcame the absence of sight and hearing to bring attention to what every human being has to offer was truly extraordinary. These three people certainly had some natural abilities but their greatness has more to do with their character and the way they responded to life's challenges.

I have been blessed to know some very gifted people with tremendous character. My mother was the rock of our family and stepped into any situation with fierce determination and selfless love to make things better. My father was a man who taught me to give my best and role modeled that commitment to excellence by working long hours to provide for our family. He then found time to use his love of music and self-taught talent to be a music director in churches for 35 years. My wife, Marcie, is one of the kindest and most sensitive people I have ever known and gives love unconditionally to everyone she meets. My daughter, Kelly, faced breast cancer as a 35-year old young woman with such courage and grace that she inspired all of us around her. My son, Chris, has the ability to build relationships that are very special and uses this gift as a coach, teacher, and minister to develop and build up others. My sister, Carolyn, was a public health nurse for 25 years and provided loving care to people who could not afford help otherwise. My sister, Betty, battled cancer courageously for seven years after being given a year to live and transformed some lives during that time. One of my best friends, Zellie, can make a group of people feel safe and very comfortable in a classroom setting and is a gifted teacher. I could name many others I've known who are outstanding in different ways.

However, as special as these people are to me, many people could identify someone they know who are equally outstanding in various ways. For example, two of the people I mentioned above were my daughter, Kelly, and my sister, Betty. They both responded to breast cancer with great courage and determination. As I went through that journey with them, I encountered many women with similar stories. This made me aware that Kelly and Betty's story was not as unique as the way Debbie has responded to the challenges in her life. To me, someone who is exceptional is that one in a million person who does truly amazing things which few other human beings have done. It involves those situations where it is difficult to imagine how the person is able to deal with that challenge so victoriously. When I look at being exceptional in that way, the conclusion I come to is that Debbie is the most exceptional person I have ever personally known. This is why I want to share her story.

In telling the story, I will first describe the tragic accident that was the beginning point for Debbie's story. The next chapter will be about the journey that Debbie took which enabled those who knew her to see evidence of this incredible person she had become. I will then explore the factors that contributed to shaping Debbie's life. Finally, I will provide some reflections on the meaning of Debbie's life in the context of our world today.

The primary sources for this story are interviews with Debbie, her father, Mac, my mother, Lockey, and other members of the family. I also gathered some memories and stories from friends. The final source is my personal observations over the last 48 years.

Chapter 2

The Accident:
A Life Changing Event

On that Saturday morning the day after New Year's Day, the phone rang and the lives of my mother's family changed forever. A morning that began in leisure and planning for a day of fun suddenly changed to one of shock and despair. My aunt, Loraine, and her two children Ronald (Butch) and Debbie, had been in a serious automobile accident. We were informed Butch had been killed; Loraine and Debbie were at the hospital. We would soon discover that Debbie was unconscious and had serious brain injuries. I will never forget the shock associated with hearing this terrible news.

It was January 2, 1965. The McDonald, Wilson,

and Toomey families had just completed a wonderful holiday season. This meant everyone had gathered in Athens for family time. Part of the celebration included time at the individual family homes for food, gifts and just sharing. Most of my cousins were still in Athens. Both of my sisters were away from Athens. My oldest sister, Carolyn was in Atlanta, Georgia with her husband, David Minor, and their 10-month old daughter, Beverly. My other sister Betty and her husband, Bob Foster, were finishing their degrees at the University of Tennessee. I was a high school senior at McMinn County High School, as was Butch.

At this time, I can't remember the specifics of that Christmas celebration and holiday season, but they were good because they always were. The celebration would have included a great Christmas cantata at our church where my father led the music. For my family it included watching numerous football games during the days when there were several major bowl games on at the same time. I can't recall where my Dad and I got the other TVs, but we would actually watch three games at a time. During those days, the Orange Bowl, Sugar Bowl, and Cotton Bowl were played at the same time. We numbered the television sets so if you saw a great play developing on the game you were watching, you could yell "look at number 2!" This was way before instant replay and SportsCenter. The gathering at our home would include Mom, Dad, Carolyn, David, Beverly, Betty, Bob, and me crowding into our small three bedroom house with one bathroom and catching up with each other, eating Mom's great food, and playing many games of Rook.

It also included the traditional family Christmas

lunch at my grandmother's home. The lives of the McDonalds, Wilsons, and Toomeys were not necessarily ideal but they were very good. One of the major reasons for that was my grandmother, Nora Wilson. She provided the heart of our family

We always had Thanksgiving and Christmas lunch at Mamaw's house, and those gatherings were and continue to be very special to me. There would be 26 people eating in this small two-bedroom house, and we would be everywhere. These family celebrations included the men rabbit hunting in the morning while the ladies prepared the food and talked. After lunch, we would watch football and just visit with each other. The day would often move into leftovers for dinner. These gatherings created some of our favorite memories growing up.

The phone call on that holiday Saturday morning brought the fun and celebration to an abrupt end. What began as a normal holiday morning of leisure and planning activities for the day became a scramble to deal with a harsh new reality that began with the terrible automobile accident.

The drive from the McDonald's farm between Athens and Decatur included crossing U.S. Route 11W which went through Virginia and Tennessee. It was a major roadway from northern states to Georgia and Florida. It was a heavily traveled road. The original 11W was a two-lane road through Athens, a small town of about 14,000 people. The new section of 11W which went around downtown Athens was a four-lane divided highway that was about nine miles long. Approximately in the middle of this section of 11W was the crossing of Tennessee state route 30 (Decatur Road). This intersection had a reputation for accidents. In the recent past, travelers on 11W had the right-of-way with a stop sign requiring people approaching the intersection on highway 30 to stop before entering the intersection. Due to the high number of accidents at this location, a traffic signal was installed which required traffic from both highways to stop when the signal was red.

The following article in the January 4, 1965 Daily Post-Athenian, described the accident:

> "McMinn High School resumed classes today but there was one student missing.

> Ronald Austin McDonald, 17 will never graduate. He died early Saturday morning from injuries received in a grinding crash at the Highway 11W by-pass and the Decatur Road intersection.

> Four others were injured, two critically, the latter being members of the same family as the deceased.

> Young McDonald was driving a 1956 Plymouth which was struck by a 1965 Buick as McDonald attempted to cross the intersection. Police reports indicated the car driven by a man from Alexandria, Virginia ran a red light and smashed into the McDonald car.

> Severely injured were McDonald's 42-year old mother, Loraine and his little four-year old sister, Debra Sue. The child was rushed on to Children's

Hospital in Chattanooga where she is suffering from a brain injury.

The driver of the other car was injured but not seriously. A passenger in the car, an 18 year-old Texas A&M student who was hitchhiking suffered face lacerations. The driver was from Cumberland, Maryland.

An Athens' policeman who investigated the accident said the driver of the car who hit the McDonald car would face manslaughter charges."

(Names of those involved other than the McDonald family were not included)

The obituary for Butch shared the following information which gives a feel for the type of young man he was:

"The son of Austin Earl and Loraine Wilson McDonald was assigned to Boyd Trew's home room at McMinn County High School. Ronald had received the Academic Letter and was a member of the Classical Club, Inter-Act Club, and the Science Club at McMinn High. Ronald was a member of Clearwater Baptist Church."

A few days after the accident, an editorial appeared in the same paper entitled "Deaths Continue". Here is an excerpt from that article:

..... "What can be done to stop the senseless automobile accidents at the intersection of Highway 11 by-pass and the Decatur Road?

It is sometimes difficult to understand why so many accidents occur at this spot. There's no blind hills on the highway. A motorist pulling out onto the island from Decatur Road can see several yards either way.

Still the accidents come.

Just last Saturday a young McMinn High Student lost his life in a two car crash at this very intersection.

Police reports indicate that the out-of-state car had run a red light, striking the local car.

While the driver, if he is guilty of ignoring a traffic light cannot be excused for breaking the law, it could be said in his defense that the light "slipped up on him."

It is a difficult light to see. And there is no warning that you are approaching a traffic light. The light dangles too high and on occasions you're under it before you realize it's there.

The Tennessee Safety Department and the Governor's office are trying to do something about the wholesale slaughter on Tennessee Highways. Last year it soared past the 1,000 mark for the first time.

Local officers would like to do something about the traffic accidents which mangle and kill.

Perhaps by working together at least one trouble spot could be eliminated.

It goes without saying that most of the trouble at the Decatur Crossing intersection would have been avoided had officials seen fit to over-pass the by-pass.

Of course it would cost a bit more money. But if it cost 100,000 and saved one life it would have been money well spent.

Until such moves are made, however, we must remedy the situation in any manner possible."

Before I reflect on the days following the accident and the impact of this tragedy on our family, I want to share a few additional details about the accident.

First of all, the family was told that the driver of the other car had been driving all night and likely fell asleep at the wheel. In addition, the impact on the McDonald car and other evidence at the scene of the crash suggested that the other car which broad-sided the car driven by Butch was possibly going about 70 miles per hour in a 45 miles per hour zone.

The year 1965 was pre-seatbelt and shoulder harnesses. The car Butch, Loraine, and Debbie were in did not have seat belts or shoulder harnesses. In fact, the first seat belt law was federal legislation which took effect on January 1, 1968. This law only required that vehicles other than buses be fitted with seat belts in all designated seating positions.

When the car ran the red light on Highway 11W, it hit the McDonald car broadside at about 70 miles per hour. The force of the collision propelled Butch through the front windshield of the car. Butch flew through the air about 20 yards and his head struck a wooden post in the median and he died instantly. Loraine was tossed from the car through the passenger side door and sustained a broken arm in several places and numerous lacerations. Debbie was thrown from the front seat to the rear passenger area and was evidently tossed about in a traumatic way. When the first responders arrived, the first one to the car initially thought Debbie was a rag doll in the back floor board. She was unconscious and the only outward evidence of injury was a black eye.

As we discovered these tragic details, it was overwhelming. For me, as a 17-year-old, this was my first experience with the death of a close family member, and it was shocking and very painful. My grandparents on my father's side of the family had died when I was a small child, and I had one of my Toomey cousins die when I was very young due to injuries in a fire accident. Those were faint memories because of the difficulty of understanding those things at an early age.

For me, the first death which raised the

awareness of the fragility and uncertainty of life was the death of John F. Kennedy a little over a year prior to the accident. I liked President Kennedy, not just because my dad was a die-hard Democrat, but because I found Kennedy to be a charismatic leader who embodied courage, had a deep sense of justice for all, and possessed a tremendous sense of humor. As a 15-year-old, I can still remember his news conferences and how he respected those who were tough on him and never took himself too seriously. I stayed glued to the TV as the events surrounding his assassination unfolded. I can remember crying because his death seemed so premature, unnecessary, and wasteful. I grieved his death and later learned about how that deep sense of loss impacts us.

Butch's death was very personal. We were the same age. We were not just cousins but friends. We had shared a lot of fun and meaningful experiences as we were growing into young men. The days following the accident are like a blur as we were in shock about Butch's death and trying to figure out what to do to help Loraine and Debbie.

I remember Loraine asking my cousin Jerry and me to stay at the funeral home the night between the evening of receiving friends and the funeral the next day. Jerry was the oldest of the four male cousins who were within about a year in age. Butch, Bill (Jerry's brother) and I were the other three. Jerry was 18 years old and I was going to be 18 in about a week. We were pretty mature for our age (I think) and were more than glad to do what Loraine wanted even though it was not easy. One of my vivid memories is of two men, whom we did not know, staying with us for a while, I'm sure with a sincere desire to help.

After about an hour, they began telling jokes in an attempt to lighten the mood. That was not what Jerry and I needed at that time. We could not go there. One trait I got from my mother is taking charge in these type situations. I told them that Jerry and I would like to be alone, and we would appreciate them leaving.

My sister, Carolyn, has a vivid memory of the devastating sadness on Mac's face at the funeral and the sense of his bearing a tremendous burden. He had to be experiencing shock, numbness and incredible sadness all at once. It is difficult to imagine the pain Mac and Loraine were experiencing at that time.

Dealing with Butch's death was very tough for our family because he was so loved and it did not seem like it was his time. Mamaw and Papaw Wilson were still living. All of their children and spouses were still living. It just didn't seem right that one of the twelve grandchildren would be the first to die on the Wilson side of our family. We experienced all of the natural responses to the death of loved ones. They included:

Shock and disbelief that it had really happened

Anger at the driver of the other car

Anger at God for allowing this tragic accident to happen

Questions about why something so terrible could happen

Intense sadness and an overwhelming

sense of loss

Confusion about what would happen now and what did all this mean

Kathy, the youngest child of Roy Wilson, Loraine's brother, was 7 at the time of the accident and so for her, like most of us cousins, this was her first experience with death and a major injury. As Kathy talked with me about the accident, she broke down in tears as she recalled her Dad assuring her that Butch was in heaven and that Debbie was badly hurt. This was so difficult for a 7-year-old or any of us to understand.

What further complicated this grieving process and dealing with things related to Butch's death was responding to the things that Loraine and Debbie needed due to their injuries. After the accident, both Loraine and Debbie were taken to Foree Hospital, one of the two hospitals in Athens.

The determination was made quickly that Debbie's needs were beyond the capability of Foree Hospital and its staff. The decision was made to send her to the Children's Hospital in Chattanooga, Tennessee, which was about 50 miles away. The staff at Foree kept Loraine and began treating her injuries. As challenging as dealing with the injuries was for Loraine, can you imagine having to lie there knowing your son had been killed and your daughter was being taken unconscious to another hospital? As a father of two, I have often wondered how she did it. Loraine would be in the hospital for the funeral of her son and unable to be there for her daughter at this critical time in her life. None of us can understand the emotional pain she must have experienced. The physical pain was nothing in comparison.

Evans Funeral Home provided the only ambulance in town to transport Debbie to Chattanooga. There was not a medical vehicle at that time to transfer patients from an Athens hospital to another one so the hearse was the vehicle used for this purpose. My mother and Aunt Leona (Roy's wife) rode in the hearse with Debbie to Chattanooga. The hearse had engine trouble and had to stop in Cleveland (which was about half way to Chattanooga), and they had to switch to another hearse.

When they arrived at Children's Hospital, a neurologist by the name of Dr. Boehm met them. Dr. Boehm would oversee Debbie's treatment and became an important part of Debbie's survival and recovery.

Debbie was initially placed in a ward but was moved to a private room so my mother and other family members could stay with her. Mom would be with her most of the time for the next two months while she was in the hospital. She took a leave from her job, and everything else became secondary to caring for Debbie. Dad and I knew we were on our own for a while, but we would have it no other way. Life went on whether it was dealing with being kicked off the basketball team (for going in for the wrong man) or other typical teenage issues. All I remember was wanting Mom to be with Debbie. My uncles, Roy and Clint, and their wives, Leona and Edna, were with Debbie as often as possible. It goes without saying Mac was there and, of course, Loraine as she recovered.

Debbie's diagnosis was a severe brain injury in the center of the brain which controlled her nervous system. She drew up into a fetal position with her knees coming up to her chin and her chest extending outward between her arms. She only straightened out after several weeks. She gritted her teeth until she had none. She had IV's in her until the veins collapsed. Her temperature was so high that she was put on an ice blanket (without any clothes on) with ice bags on top of her. The windows were opened and the heat turned off despite it being a cold January.

At that time, oxygen tents were used and we would unzip the tent a little and reach in and pet her even though she gave no signs of recognition. Her only movement was a sucking motion with her mouth. After her veins collapsed, her jaws were clamped together so hard we couldn't feed her with a spoon. Feeding was accomplished with a premature baby bottle nipple. Later the staff started using a syringe to squirt baby food in her mouth. After about 6 weeks her muscles had relaxed some and her primary nurse, Becky Wooden, who hated feeding her with the syringe, started feeding her with a spoon. Debbie would not let anyone else do it but Becky. They would call Becky at her home during the day so she could come and feed Debbie.

Here are Becky's memories of caring for Debbie:

"While working as a nurse at the Children's Hospital in Chattanooga in 1965 I had the privilege of caring for Debbie just after the accident. She had suffered such severe brain damage that her entire body was rigid. I could pick up her foot and the rest of her body would lift up also. Her Aunt Lockey was with her most of the time. She is a Godly lady, and was such an inspiration to me as I watched her so lovingly care for Debbie during this time. God knit our hearts together in a beautiful friendship that has lasted all of these many years. One night when I entered the room she was standing over looking out of the window; I could tell that something was really troubling her. She shared with me that Dr. Boehm had told her that Debbie would probably not live, and if she did she would be like a vegetable. She said to me, 'I just can't go home and tell them (her parents) that – I just can't do it.' We prayed and she decided that indeed she would not go home and tell them that because no one knew what Debbie's future would be.

Debbie was in an oxygen tent and received intravenous fluids for several weeks. After a period of time, the doctor decided that we would try to give her some pureed food. The day shift would put this in a Dakin's syringe and gently press it into her mouth. I worked the 3-11 shifts and had a little more time to devote to feeding her, so I decided to try to feed her with a spoon. I also decided that while I was feeding her I would sing to her so she could get used to the sound of my voice. Soooooo I unzipped the oxygen tent, got just inside of the tent, and began my singing and feeding! Bless her little heart; she was able to take that nourishment from a spoon. In fact, she got spoiled to that, because soon after that she would not eat from anyone but me! I was even called on my days off to see if I had time to come by and feed her since she refused to eat for the other nurses! Somehow I always managed to find the time to go by the hospital and feed her lunch to her. What a sweet problem to have!

In late February or early March, I left Chattanooga and moved to Memphis to go back to school. Debbie was still in a coma when I left, but began to respond after that and was able to be discharged before I went home for the first time. I had stayed in touch with Lockey and knew that Debbie was gradually beginning to respond more. I was so anxious to see her and see the progress she was making, so during that first trip home I went to Athens to see for myself. She was on the front porch in a wheelchair when I got there but they had not told her that I was coming. When I leaned over and spoke her name, she grinned real big and said, 'Becky'. I don't think there was a dry eye on the porch. All of that singing paid off and she recognized me by my voice! What excitement we all felt! In the next few years I went several times to see her, and kept up with her through Lockey."

Becky's amazement at Debbie's progress is easy to understand in light of the severity of her injuries. Dr. Boehm and the other doctors who treated Debbie did not think she would leave the hospital alive. When we hung on to the hope of her living, they would temper our optimism with the statements that if she did live, she would probably never be able to live a normal life. The brain damage was so severe that the doctors in their best medical judgment could not foresee a good outcome.

During that first month after the accident, Mac and Loraine were left with the death of their son and the possible death of their little daughter. They also had to deal with the possibility that if Debbie survived, she would live in a vegetative state. It was impossible for the family to imagine the pain of those events and it still is. In spite of the assurance of Butch's destiny, the verse that was in the Memory Pamphlet at Butch's funeral reflected the feelings they must have had.

There is never life without sadness

There is never a heart free from pain;

If one seeks in this world for true solace,

He seeks it forever in vain

So when to your heart comes the sorrow

Of losing some dear one you've known

Tis the touch of God's sickle at the harvest

Since He reaps in the fields What He has sown.

Those feelings of grief, of course, continued for some time. I discovered a Christmas card Loraine wrote to Butch, her deceased son, a year after his death. The verse in the card was:

I'd like to be with you today

If only for a while

I'd like to share your company

And see your cheery smile

But since that seems impossible

I'll do the next best thing

And visit you in heart and thought

By just remembering

At the end of this verse, Loraine wrote: To Butch from your Mother, Christmas, 1965.

After being in the hospital two months, Debbie didn't need oxygen anymore and she began to relax. Dr. Boehm sent her home expecting her to basically remain in that condition. Although we all clung to the hope for more, it was difficult to do so.

Chapter 3

Debbie's Incredible Life

The Recovery

After the accident, Loraine, Mac and Debbie moved in with Mamaw Wilson. This would enable them to be a few houses away from my mom and closer to the rest of the family. The early years of Debbie's recovery would require the support of the entire family and everyone responded. Helping Debbie recover was a major focus for everyone. Remember, the prognosis was dim. The doctors, based on the medical evidence, indicated that a meaningful life for Debbie was not in the cards. We all refused to accept that outcome.

Mac, Loraine, and the rest of the family simply began to act. Each day we did what we could to help her get better whether it was: talking to her and touching her even though she would not respond; exercising her arms and legs even though we were told she would never be able to use them; planning the next step even though progress was not supposed to happen; and, of course praying. We prayed, believing that God had a purpose and plan for Debbie even though there was no evidence for that. Entire churches would have special prayer during Sunday and Wednesday services in addition to a lot of individual prayers. Years after the accident, Uncle Clint expressed it well. He said that he believed God altered the course of Debbie's life and enabled her to live because God saw what a blessing Deb could be to other people because of her attitude and how she could bring Glory to Him.

When she left the hospital they found she had a broken bone in her upper leg from drawing up into a knot so they put on a cast. At that point she could look around but couldn't speak. At this time we fed her with a spoon like a baby, and we carried her around like an infant. The only response we observed was after about two months at home, she would follow us with her eyes. Mom would tell me about talking to Debbie when she was bathing her and encouraging her to say Mama. Debbie eventually started trying to say Mama and other words and slowly began smiling and talking like a baby does.

Six weeks after Debbie came home from the hospital, she went back to see Dr. Boehm for a follow-up visit. When Mac carried her into his office, Debbie looked at the doctor and smiled and tears flowed down both his cheeks. He declared "It's a miracle! It's a miracle!" Dr. Boehm could not believe that she was responding to the people around her. This was tremendous news to him but there were many challenges ahead.

Not long after this, Debbie was taken back to her orthopedist to take the cast off, but in doing so her hip broke because her bones were so sensitive from the brain damage and her drawing up. She went back into a cast which extended from under her arms to her ankles. Her legs were spread apart with a broom handle connected to each ankle. We had to turn her sideways to carry her through doors. She had to wear the cast for a year. As we would exercise Debbie, we had to do so with great care because her bones were so fragile that they could break easily. During this time, Debbie was not talking very much. As we would do physical therapy with her, we would ask her to blink if we were hurting her.

During the early years of her recovery, she experienced numerous surgeries and physical challenges. She had to have a rod put in her back to prevent it from bending. She had knee surgery. One effect of the brain damage was that the bones on one side of her body did not grow in the same way as the other. As a result, it was necessary to remove a section of one leg so it would be close to the same length as the leg which was not growing normally. She had to be in a body cast due to breaking her hip during normal body movement. She also broke her arm in a similar way. In addition, she had pneumonia due to being so immobile during this time. The brain damage also affected her speech, and she received speech therapy to enable her to communicate more effectively.

After renting a home on Jones Street two houses up from Mamaw Wilson for a brief time, Loraine and Mac bought and moved into a house next door to my mom and dad in 1966. This was right up the street from Mamaw Wilson. My mom had returned to work but her calling was helping with Debbie. She would walk home from work at lunch to see Debbie and would visit several times a day to help in various ways. Part of Debbie's physical therapy was swimming. On the back of Loraine and Mac's house, they built a concrete block pool that was about 12 feet square and about 4 feet deep. Mom and Debbie would get in there on any reasonably warm day and exercise.

About a year after the accident, it became apparent Debbie would not live a vegetative life. She increasingly interacted and responded to the people and things around her. She was like a young child learning words for the first time but she was a fast learner and began to talk quickly. What a miracle!

Debbie would talk very fast during that time. Her speech was impaired which made it difficult to understand her. A speech therapist worked with her, but it was difficult for anyone who did not have regular contact with Debbie to comprehend what she was saying. I was away in college at the time. When I would come home and visit Debbie, Loraine would repeat things when she felt I did not understand.

As Debbie regained her vocabulary and began communicating with us, we began to see a new Debbie in many ways. The shy and timid little girl we remembered was coming out of her shell. Debbie loved to talk with people. She always wanted to know what was going on with each of us. She loved to hear about the things that were happening in other people's lives. She found joy in the things other people were doing even though many of those activities were obviously beyond what she could physically do.

She also loved to tell us about the things she was doing. We were always amazed at how sweet Debbie was in spite of everything. She always had a smile and made us feel like seeing us had made her day.

We also were able to confirm that the bright little girl we observed prior to the accident was still there. The accident had not robbed her of any mental functioning. Her cousin, Kathy, remembers staying with Mamaw as a young child (which we all did and loved) and at some point in the day, Mamaw would jump up and say, "It's Debbie time." Mamaw and whoever was there would go see Debbie and play games. Kathy remembers that Debbie won most the time.

Another thing that appeared was an incredible sense of humor. Here was someone who was battling physically everyday and limited in the things she could do and she still found within herself a love for laughter. Every time I visited we would talk about how Mom's feet stank (they didn't, but that was irrelevant). I would bring it up and Debbie and I would both go, "shoo."

Mac and Loraine never talked about Butch and after the accident they did not tell Debbie about Butch until she was in her late 40's. They were very protective of Debbie and tried to minimize the pain she experienced whether physical or emotional.

When they finally decided to tell her about Butch's death, Debbie's response was a classic. She looked at them and said, "Do I have any other brothers or sisters that you are not telling me about?" Her response was not in anger or frustration. Her response was a great example of her sense of humor and her ability to take life as it is. After learning about Butch, she would always want to talk about him, and it was wonderful to be able to relive our wonderful memories of Butch. Debbie as usual focused on the good of those memories and not the fact that she had not had the joy of having a brother for the last 40-plus years.

The medical challenges were constant. The brain damage had affected the way Debbie's bones developed on one side of her body but it did not affect the resolve with which the faced the challenges associated with that problem. When it was necessary to remove a section of the bone in the developing leg to shorten it so it would be a similar length to the other leg, she took it in stride. It was incredible that we never saw her down emotionally. We would get discouraged at times but Debbie would just accept those setbacks and make the best of every situation.

As the physical setbacks diminished, Debbie was able to walk a little with some help. She loved to move and do things. With some nudging from my mom, Loraine, Mac, Debbie, and my mother would go on outings. They loved to go to some special places to eat. They also enjoyed going to Watts Bar Lake for picnics. We never had to ask Debbie to go somewhere twice. She was always ready. She seemed fearless.

It is important to note that every activity for

Debbie was difficult. She could not stand, walk or sit by herself. Her hands and fingers were drawn and doing most activities requiring manual dexterity was difficult or impossible. This meant Loraine, Mac and family members who helped at times needed to provide a lot of assistance. It was a joy to provide that assistance, but it is important to recognize that Debbie, in particular, and Loraine and Mac faced significant challenges every day. All of us close to the situation grew to have incredible respect for all of them. They were an inspiration to us, and it was almost impossible to get down and feel sorry for ourselves without thinking about Debbie's smile and positivity in the midst of terrible adversity.

School Years

When Debbie was nine years old, the decision was made for her to begin home schooling. Her home-school teacher was a dear lady by the name of Ozelle Powers. Mrs. Powers was a home-bound teacher and her husband, Prof, was a beloved principal at one of the local elementary schools and a Boy Scout leader in the community. Mrs. Powers would be Debbie's teacher for the next nine years. I asked Mrs. Powers to describe her teaching experience with Debbie.

"Debbie McDonald was one of my first home-bound students. I was the only home-bound teacher for the Athens City Schools for 17 years.

It was a pleasure to go to the McDonald house three times a week (one hour each time) for the nine years that Debbie was a student. Debbie was so sweet and friendly, and I really enjoyed her. She started in the first grade and stayed through the ninth grade.

Debbie always had her lessons and was prompt with them. She always had a smile and was so cheerful. She always wanted to know how I was when I came for a visit. She was interested in my other students and asked about them all the time.

Her parents were lovely people. They wanted Debbie to try new things and to learn what she could. They were very helpful and looked after her with much care. I know that at times it was hard to get her up, get her dressed and ready for school, but she was always ready and had a big smile. She never complained about anything.

Debbie learned the alphabet when in the first grade and she progressed each year in her vocabulary. She could do the work with ease and seemed to love doing it. She wanted to learn and really tried hard.

When she was in the 9th grade and finished she got a certificate which made her so happy. She wanted to go on to high school in home bound, but

I'm not sure if she did so.

It has been 25 (3/2012) years since I retired from teaching and I still remember her and send her birthday presents and Christmas presents each year. She was a favorite of mine and I loved her. I'm so glad I had the privilege to be her teacher for all those years!"

Debbie did go on to get her high school certificate. She had two homebound high school teachers, but I have not been able to locate them. With Debbie's intelligence, she could have gone on to college or other educational pursuits but never chose to pursue other formal education.

She loved learning and reading and over the years she read the Bible through several times. She also enjoyed music and listens to gospel music for hours each day. The Gaither family were her favorite musicians. She took great delight in watching game shows on TV. I always thought her love for these shows is evidence of her thirst for learning.

Adult Years

In discussing Debbie's adult years, we will focus on three time periods. The first I want to share are the years from 1983 through 2006. These years cover the time after she finished high school until she moved into an assisted living facility in 2006. For those years, she lived in the same home on Jones Street next to the home where I grew up.

A lot of things happened over those years. Mamaw Wilson died. This was a significant loss for Debbie, but she took that in stride as she did everything. There were, as well, lots of additions to the family as all 12 cousins married and began adding to their families.

My father died in 1989, and this was significant because Mom had always devoted a lot of attention to Debbie. Now she had even more time to give. Carolyn and I lived a good distance from Athens, and Betty was back in Athens, but much of Mom's life revolved around Debbie.

Debbie embraced everyone and everyone embraced Debbie. We all have our memories of interactions with Debbie and they always bring a smile and often a laugh. One of her cousins-in-law, Judy, says that for years, every time she would see Debbie, the question was "How's Kenny, (Judy's husband) and is he still as mean as ever?" Debbie loves Kenny and loves joking with and about him.

I always felt blessed after I visited Debbie. She always greeted me with a huge smile and a big "hi" followed by a "have a seat." She was always so inviting and in that moment I always felt like I was the most important person in the world to her. She always wanted to know what was happening in my life and would always ask about the important people in my life. She would ask questions about things that I had told her in a previous visit which was evidence, not only, of her incredible memory but her attentiveness to and caring about the things I shared with her.

To illustrate both the power of her memory and the strength of her caring for others, I want to move forward to a story from March, 2012. My mother had moved to live with my wife and me in Kingsport, Tennessee, which is about a two-and a-half hour drive from Athens. She was 91-years old at the time and could not make frequent trips to see Debbie, but we would go to Athens about every three months. We decided to plan a visit at a time that Becky Wooden Cook, the nurse mentioned earlier who helped take care of Debbie in the Children's Hospital during the weeks after the accident, could go. Although Becky had seen Debbie a few times following the accident, she had not seen Debbie or Mom for over 40 years.

We met Becky at the Cracker Barrel in Athens, and neither Mom nor I recognized her immediately. We then drove to see Debbie. When we arrived at the nursing home, we saw her in a dining hall and walked over to her. She saw us and began to smile and say "Hi." Mom leaned down and said we had brought someone to see her and asked if she knew who it was. Even though we had kept this a secret in order to surprise Debbie, she looked up and said, "It's Becky Wooden." After 40 years of not seeing Becky, she still knew this was the Becky, the only one who could feed her in those days after the accident. Later as we talked, Becky asked her if she remembered who she had married over 40 years ago and Debbie did not hesitate in responding "Jim Cook." We were all amazed. When Debbie knows someone, she takes knowing that person seriously.

The second thing we could bank on with Debbie when we came to visit was her response when asked,

"How are you doing?" This, for us southerners, is a greeting that we often use with no expectation of a response. It is more like a "hello" than a real question. I recall the frustration one of my Dutch work colleagues shared about Americans coming to the Netherlands and saying "how are you doing" and then not taking the time to listen to the response which my Dutch friends would begin to give to the question.

When we who are close to Debbie ask her how she is doing, it is more than just a greeting. We really want to know how she is doing. At times in the past when we asked the question, we knew from Loraine, Mac, or Mom that Debbie was experiencing pain, disappointment, or some form of adversity. However, without exception Debbie's response is "I'm fine." It is always said with conviction and not just as a rote response. It is said with a real smile and not a fake one. It is said with such sincerity and genuineness.

Often, I thought she can't be doing fine because I measured her condition in physical, circumstantial, and temporary terms. However, over the years I realized that Debbie had a life view that was deeper, more substantive, and certainly more spiritually centered. When Debbie says she is fine, she means it. She is fine because she is with family and friends she loves and she is able to abide in those moments. She finds joy in her relationship with God and not things of this world. She chooses everyday to look for the good in life and not be distracted or brought down by the bad.

I asked Debbie what she liked most about life. Her response was, "everything and everybody." Debbie has this incredible ability to find the positive in things. What is even more amazing is that I asked her what she would change if she could. Her response was "nothing." In Debbie we all see this incredible ability to take life as it comes and find the good in it without question, challenge, or discontent. Debbie is a living testimony to a life lived loving God and being called according to His purpose. Romans 8:28 says, *"And we know that in all things God works for the good of those who love him, who have been called according to his purpose."* Gradually I began to realize that for Debbie all things do work together for good. Debbie finds joy and the good in every experience of life whether it is her life changing injuries, the physical limitations of her life, Butch's death, her mother's death, or whatever life deals her.

Mac told me that anytime Debbie was confronted with anything that was troubling or sad she would respond after a moment of reflection with, "well." It seemed she would then process the sad or troubling thing and put it in perspective. She would then respond in words and actions in ways that were wise and filled with hope.

Debbie has a passion for life and is always open to new experiences. As I mentioned, she loves to go places and do things. Loraine, Mac, Mom, and Debbie were always going out to do things. Loraine and Mac would make sure they got out almost every day for something even if Mom couldn't go.

My sister, Betty, taught her to play a piano even though it is very difficult for Debbie to move her fingers. It seems that Debbie isn't afraid to try anything. I often think of the passage from 1 John 4:18 in relation to Debbie. That verse says, *"There is no fear in love: but perfect love casteth out fear, because fear hath punishment; and he that feareth is not made perfect in love."* Debbie's love seems to be as close to a perfect one as I have ever seen in another person and so it is not surprising that fear seems to be cast out of her.

Home to Assisted Living

In 2006, my sister, Betty, died after a 7-year battle with breast cancer. This was a tremendous blow to our family, and it was so unexpected. It also seemed very unfair because she lived such a healthy lifestyle. She never smoked, was a healthy eater, exercised regularly, and looked almost like she did when she graduated from high school. Betty was 55 at the time of the diagnosis and was given less than a year to live. She faced surgery, chemo, lifestyle changes, changes of appearance, and pain with such dignity and courage. During that time, Betty and her husband, Bob, spent a great deal of time with her children and grandchildren. They took a dream trip to Israel. The most important thing she did was renew a relationship with a granddaughter that had been estranged due to the actions of a former daughter-in-law. This beautiful young lady now has a wonderful relationship with her father and our entire family. This would have probably never happened without the dogged determination of Betty to make something "right" before she went on to be with her Lord. She was such an inspiration to our family and her many friends. At that time my mom was 86-years old and still living next door to the

McDonald family. Mom's ability to help physically was limited at this time as she co-battled the cancer with Betty, but she was still a major source of moral support. As I reflect on the way Betty and Mom dealt with Betty's cancer, it is just another illustration of the faith, hope, and love that is available to people of faith. Debbie draws on that every day and it is easy to see that same faith making a difference around her each day.

When Betty died, Debbie was 45-years old and Mac was 87 and Loraine was 84. Due to the deteriorating health of both Mac and particularly Loraine, it was becoming more and more apparent that the McDonalds could not live in an independent living situation. A major concern of Mom and everyone was what the long-term future would be for Debbie. My Mom was a master caregiver, and she always felt a sense of responsibility to take care of others and situations even if they were not her responsibility. Debbie was like a daughter to Mom in some ways and she worried a great deal about her.

She began talking with Loraine and Mac about exploring the possibility of moving into an assisted living situation. This is a difficult decision for many, and it was particularly difficult for them. They did begin looking at facilities and finally chose to move to one in Sweetwater, TN, which was about 10 miles from Athens. This particular facility provided a small room and bath for Mac and a similar room for Loraine and Debbie. The rooms were right across from each other. They kept their home and clung to the possibility that they would be able to return.

Mom felt good about this living situation for the three of them. After Betty's death, we began talking with Mom about moving in with us. Though Mom had told us that she would never move in with any of her children, she finally decided to do so. With my other sister, Carolyn, and her husband in Louisville, KY and Marcie and I in Kingsport, TN (about 150 miles from Athens), we felt she needed to be close to one of us. Our situation made the most sense, so we added a large room with a private bath for Mom on to our house and she came to live with us in July of 2007. We had five wonderful years of Mom living with us, and she died a peaceful death on August 22, 2012 in our home.

The most difficult thing about leaving Athens for Mom was not being able to see Debbie often. We would make trips to Sweetwater every few months to see Debbie and her mom and dad. My mom found great peace knowing Debbie had a safe and caring new home.

It is easy to underestimate the significance of this move for Debbie and her parents. First of all the only home that Debbie really remembers in a significant way is her home on Jones Street next to our house. She had lived there for almost 40 years.

In addition to the physical adjustment to a new home, think about the emotional one. Debbie had been living in this safe little cocoon of family and a few dear friends for 40 years. Other than medical staff, three homebound teachers and encounters with strangers in restaurants, every relationship Debbie had was with family members. She had never had to deal with other students whether they were friends or bullies. She had never been in the workplace and experienced the satisfaction of having a great colleague or the necessity of addressing a conflict with co-workers. She had not been a part of a Sunday School class nor had the opportunity to choose what friend she wanted to sit with in worship. She had never had the opportunity to live a normal day-to-day life and have the opportunity to have fun with a broad range of people and make new friendships.

All of a sudden Debbie was in a new home where she would need to interact with caregivers other than her family every day. She would be having lunch each day in a dining hall with a group of people she had never met. If she chose to participate in scheduled activities like worship, games, crafts, and music, she would be doing those things with people who were new acquaintances.

This would be overwhelming for many people coming from Debbie's background. However, it was like watching a blooming flower. She blossomed in ways that amazed us all. Debbie immediately made friends with everyone who lived and worked there. She sought people out and got to know them. Even though it was initially difficult for them to understand her due to Debbie's speech impediment, this did not deter her. Gradually, everyone grew to love Debbie. They loved her sense of humor. They loved her smile. They loved how she was always positive and took a genuine interest in them.

We were amazed in some ways and not in others. This was the same Debbie we knew but it was still hard to comprehend how she made it seem so easy.

Debbie became a leader in the facility. The staff actually put a sign on her door saying "Assistant Craft Manager." When going into any social setting, it is easy to tell who the heart and soul of the group is.

Debbie was that person. It was easy to see Debbie was loved, and Debbie loved them.

As Christmas was approaching one year, Mom wanted to do something special for the staff there because they were so good to Debbie. Mom was an incredible seamstress and made things for most of the women in our family through the years including wedding and prom dresses. Due to deteriorating eyesight, she was not able to do that but she could still crochet and make necklaces and bracelets with beads. She asked Debbie if she would like to give all the staff members a necklace or bracelet. Debbie got so excited about that because it was a way she could show her love and appreciation to the staff. Mom made the necklaces, and a few weeks before Christmas, we visited Debbie and spent an hour determining which necklace would be given to which staff member. It was very personal for Debbie. We then put them in bags with name tags and Debbie gave them to each of the staff members at Christmas.

This time in Sweetwater was not as easy for Loraine and Mac. They longed to go home. At one point, they said they were going to try to get well enough to move back home. Debbie told them they could go if they wanted to but she was staying, and she meant it. No one loved their parents more than Debbie, but she loved being around lots of people with lots of things to do. Debbie learned to play games on a computer. She loved the stimulation of doing things with other people and trying new experiences.

I remember telling Mom after one of our visits that Debbie had been an adult for years and we were just now recognizing it. She was able to make decisions for herself. She was able to develop relationships on her own. She also, as well as any human being I've ever known, understood who she was and what she wanted and was quite capable, despite her many limitations, of going after what she wanted.

In fact, she sometimes stretched those limits a little too far. One example of this was when she wanted to visit the Big K down the road to get something and no one had the time to take her. Shortly after she moved to the assisted-living facility, Debbie got a motorized wheel chair called a jazzy. Just like her new home freed Debbie up emotionally and relationally, the jazzy freed her in some ways physically. Now Debbie could move about on her own without the assistance of others. Well, she demonstrated that quite well when she wanted to go to the Big K. When no one noticed, Debbie left the facility and began going down the road to the Big K, which was about a mile away. When someone finally realized Debbie had gone, they got in the van and went after her and then took her to the Big K.

This shows the incredible determination and courage of this young lady. Debbie is more focused on what she can do than what she can't do. It is always about the possibilities of each moment and not the limitations.

It became obvious after about two years that Loraine and Debbie would need more caregiving than that facility could provide. Debbie's physical limitations and the demands of attending to them required more of a nursing home environment. Loraine had hip surgery during this time and had a difficult recovery. This required her to go back and forth between a hospital and a nursing home.

Woods Memorial Nursing Home

Eventually, it became necessary for Loraine to go into a nursing home, and the decision was made that she would go to Woods Memorial Nursing Home in Etowah, TN., which is about five miles from Athens. In the past, Mom would have been an important part of that decision-making process. Since Mom had moved to Kingsport, Mac's younger brother, Bill (16 years younger), and his wife, Dixie, had taken over that role of helping with decisions related to Debbie's care.

Bill and Dixie did a great job of helping with the decisions and making arrangements that Mac, Loraine, and Debbie were unable to deal with anymore. From our perspective, they were a God-send. Bill and Dixie played a critical role in choosing Woods Memorial as the best care-giving situation for Loraine, and that decision proved to be one which would be a major blessing for Debbie.

Shortly after Loraine went to live at Woods on a permanent basis, it was necessary to move Debbie there also. During the early days at Woods, a major part of her focus was attending to her mom. You could see that she fit right in immediately just as she did in Sweetwater. Loraine did not do nearly as well. Many of us would struggle in that environment. Most people cringe at the thought of living in a nursing home. Few of us would choose that alternative. My wife, sister, sister-in-law, her husband, and I took every action we could take to help our parents avoid that and we were blessed to be able to do so.

With this in mind, each time Mom and I visited Loraine and then Debbie, Mom and I would leave Woods with a heavy heart in some ways because they had to be in that environment. However, we also came away with thanksgiving because Woods Memorial Nursing Home is a wonderful residential facility. It is obvious the staff cares for their residents and they work hard to make it a clean, attractive, and pleasant place to be. We knew this was to be Loraine's home for a short while, but it would likely be Debbie's home for a much longer time. Knowing Debbie was in a good place was important to all of the family, but Mom would have had no peace of mind if she had thought that Debbie was not in a loving, safe and healthy place. Woods gave Mom that peace of mind.

In January of 2011, Mom and I received a call from Dixie telling us that Debbie had pneumonia and she was in Woods Memorial Hospital, which was attached to the nursing home. Before we could prepare to leave for Athens to see Debbie, we received another call indicating Loraine was in critical condition. We quickly left for Athens. As we approached Athens, we received a call informing us that Loraine had died suddenly. It was decided that Mom and I would go to the hospital and tell Debbie about her mother's death. I have been in that situation as a family member and a minister, and it is never easy.

We arrived in Debbie's room, and we talked to

the nurses to be sure Debbie was physically able to have that conversation. Debbie's response to being told about her mother's death was one of those moments demonstrating the exceptional character of this unique person. When Mom told her, I will never forget watching Debbie bow her head for a moment and then look up and say, "Now Mom can see and walk again." Paul wrote to the church at Philippi in Philippians 1:21: *"For to me to live is Christ, and to die is gain."* Debbie's response to her mother's death is testimony to her belief and faith in the truth of this verse. Debbie was closer to her mom than any other human being, and they had a deep love for each other and an interdependency for over 40 years. However, Debbie's faith in God enabled her to see the positive and gain associated with this personal loss. For Debbie, it always seems more about God first and others second and so she simply responded in the way she always does. Debbie was "fine." Wow. Loraine had been the rock by Debbie's side for 50 years, and that loss to Debbie was secondary to the fact that her mother did not have to suffer or be limited in any way for another day. She was now with her heavenly Father and was now whole. Such wisdom and selflessness.

Of course Debbie grieves like any human being will. Debbie Oswald, a nurse at Woods Memorial the entire time Debbie has been there, indicated she has only seen Debbie "down" on a few occasions. She identified the days following her mother's death and serious illnesses Debbie has experienced as examples of those times. Ms. Oswald quickly pointed out, however, that even during those painful experiences Debbie tried to remain positive, sweet and joyful.

Although the transition to Woods was difficult and the death of Loraine was a major loss, it was easy to see that Debbie had found a real home. Debbie always says she loves everything and everybody, and that is apparent in her new home. She embraced the staff, residents and lifestyle in the nursing home and made things joyful. After she recovered from the pneumonia for which she was hospitalized during the time around Loraine's death and funeral, she was taken back to the nursing home and the staff told us she burst through the double doors in her jazzy and with enthusiasm exclaimed, "I'm back!"

It quickly became common knowledge for all who visited Debbie that it is pointless going to her room to find her because she is always out visiting others and participating in activities. So when we arrive, we tell a staff member we are there to see Debbie. Without exception the staff member will laugh and say "Well she's around here somewhere," and then they will proceed to roam the halls until they find Debbie. In a few minutes, Debbie will come into the dining area on her jazzy with that big smile and "hi". Of course, one of us will say "How are you doing?" Then with a big smile, Debbie will respond with "I'm fine."

Visits there always lift our spirits because we can see how happy Debbie is. She always tells us about some wonderful things she has done. Those things include: playing bingo and other group games; attending gospel and other concerts they have at the nursing home; going on field trips to museums or out to eat; and, funny things that have happened. Debbie is always ready for anything whether it's enjoying animals that people bring to the nursing home or planting flowers to make the outside look more beautiful.

Woods does a great job of planning activities and celebrating special events. It is always decorated for the season. One time when we visited around St. Patrick's Day, Debbie came to greet us wearing a hat with four-leaf clovers on wires bouncing around her head. At Christmas time, she always has on Christmas attire. Debbie's love of life bubbles over.

It is obvious that Kim Rucker, the Activities' Director, loves Debbie. She laughed as she told me how Debbie keeps everyone on their toes. She said Debbie continually says "We need more trips, bingo, and singers." Kim responds, "Debbie we're working ourselves to death planning and doing these activities." Debbie's response was, "All I know is we need more activities."

Debbie also helps to make sure everything runs the way it is supposed to run. One time a singing group did not show up on a Sunday they were scheduled to sing. Kim was not there that day, but when she came to work Monday morning Debbie informed her about the group not being there and told her that this should not happen because everyone was looking forward to hearing them. She told Kim she needed to call to determine what happened and bugged her until she got to the bottom of this problem.

Kim also shared how when guest singers or speakers come, Debbie is always at the door to greet them and then she drives her jazzy to the front row. She sings along with the singers because she seems to know the words to every song and always sings the loudest. When the singers or speakers leave,

Debbie goes with them to the door and says good bye and invites them back. One group has come once a month ever since Debbie has been there, and they told my sister Carolyn that they come for Debbie. They love her and if Debbie is not at the door to greet them, they want to know where she is. The visitors call her "the greeter." She has fun with this role. One day out of the blue she started going down the halls saying "Welcome to Walmart" and laughing. It brought laughter and smiles to everyone in a place where smiles and laughter are not always easy to come by.

The activity director's children love to come to Woods and do Bible quizzes, but it is not a fair contest because they have found that Debbie knows the answer to every question. Debbie loves to win and always brings enthusiasm to every game. I shared a story about Debbie remembering Becky Wooden Cook's husband's name with one of the nurses and she confirmed that Debbie has an incredible memory. She seems to forget nothing. A lot of this is a testimony to how bright Debbie is but a lot of it is how she soaks in every word, name, person, and event she experiences. She loves life and lives it with great intensity, moment to moment. To illustrate this zest for life, Kim said Debbie doesn't want to go to sleep at night because she might miss something, and she literally "runs" around all day until the battery in her jazzy runs out.

I've been in institutional settings like Woods Memorial where I could sense the staff saw the residents as a burden they were carrying. I've never felt that at Woods. In fact with Debbie, I am confident the staff genuinely loves and even admires her. Evidence of this is the fact that the staff members who make Debbie's bed everyday take great pains in placing all 54 of her stuffed animals in the "right place." Debbie sleeps each night amongst those stuffed animals. It is difficult not to do a little extra for Debbie when it is obvious how Debbie goes out of her way every day to show love and kindness to others. Debbie always greets people with a smile, and she knows the names of all the staff and residents. She goes out of her way every day to visit with as many as she can, and everyone laughs because it starts from the time she gets up. She is literally out in the halls greeting everyone.

One staff member said Debbie is the sunshine in everyone's day. I saw evidence of this the time Mom and I visited with Becky Wooden Cook. We were standing around a table in the dining hall visiting with Debbie, and I noticed a lady at the next table watching Debbie and smiling. I greeted her and asked how she was doing. She said she was doing well and then added, "Debbie is the one who keeps us going."

Ms. Oswald told me that as soon as Debbie hears anyone moving around in the morning, she says "Good morning" to let everyone know she is ready for the day. Debbie loves life and approaches every day with a positivity that insures every day will be a good day. She finds joy in big and small things and every interaction with another person.

Chapter 4

What Made the Difference

When I examine the life of someone who is one of those "one in a million" and truly extraordinary people, a question always comes to mind, "What contributed to this person being so extraordinary?" In this chapter, I want to share with you who Debbie identified as the difference makers in her life.

I interviewed Debbie the week before I started this book and I wanted to get her perspective on her life and the important influences that shaped the person she had become. I asked "who are the most influential people in your life?" Her response was God, Mom, and Dad. I asked her who helped her the most when she needed help. Her response was God, Mom, and Dad. I asked her who had taught her the most about how to live life. Want to guess what her response was? Right, it was God, Mom, and Dad. On occasion, she would add "Aunt Lockey." It was obvious that the key factors in this extraordinary life were God first, and then her mom and dad and finally my mom.

The McDonald Family

To understand the significance of Debbie's life, it is important to know the members of her family. These are such critical players in Debbie's story and knowing them helps in appreciating their response to the event that would forever change all of their lives and in particular Debbie's.

Debbie was the second child of Loraine and Austin McDonald, or Mac as we all called him. The first child was Ronald Austin McDonald, "Butch" to all of his family and friends. Butch was born in 1947 and Debbie was born in 1961. The late addition of Debbie to this family created a very different dynamic which we will explore later.

Mac was a prisoner of war in World War II. When he returned to Athens, it did not take long for Mac and Loraine to discover each other. Mac was downtown one day and saw Loraine. He told some friends that this was the person he was going to marry. He contacted her through friends and she ended another relationship, which was more of a casual friendship, in order to date Mac. This was in 1945 and they married in 1946.

Farming was important in Mac's early years and

would later help him stay alive as a POW. Mac and Loraine moved to a farm as soon as possible. They worked the farm in addition to Mac working another full-time job. Loraine stopped working when Butch was born. Mac worked at Mayfield Dairy Farms in their milk processing and shipping. Their farm was a favorite place for the male cousins to visit. We loved making the ten-mile ride there on our bikes and spending the night. We would help milk the cows and enjoyed fishing in the pond and playing on the farm.

The farm life seemed to be the perfect life for the McDonalds. Mac was an exceptional gardener and a master at living off the land. Loraine loved being a mother and homemaker. Loraine, Mac, Butch, and Debbie were all very humble and shy people, so the solitude of the farm life fit them well.

They all seemed very happy with this lifestyle. Butch was a great help to his father in working the farm. Prior to Debbie's birth, Butch was a little over-protected in the minds of many in the family. The three cousins who were close to Butch in age all lived on Jones Street in Athens. Butch would often come in to town to visit us. We city boys were used to playing on the creek behind our houses, exploring caves in the hills around our homes, playing football, and typical "boy stuff."

Weather did not matter. We did this in the snow and on the hottest of days. We did it at times when physical injury was not unlikely. Our parents were not negligent, but they did let boys be boys. At times, we would try to include Butch, but Loraine would often not let him participate. In some ways Loraine and Mac were probably exercising good judgment, but at times it seemed to be excessive to us boys. We thought Butch could have handled it because he, after all, did work on the farm.

When Debbie came along, Butch was 14 and that apparent over-protection seemed to change. Butch flourished in many ways. He was given much more freedom to do things with his cousins and friends. This resulted in his coming out of his shell, and we saw this, in particular, as it related to his involvement in high school life. Butch was very bright and became involved in several clubs and in leadership roles.

All of the family memories of Debbie in her first four years were of this beautiful, bright and shy little girl. When the family would get together, we would joke with her and she would smile and go to Butch, her mom, or dad.

Mac described Debbie as a lively little girl. She loved the farm and liked to sit on a bull and play with her big dog, Cleo. Loraine would keep her busy in the kitchen and doing needlepoint. Butch petted her and took good care of her.

Taking care of and protecting each other was a major theme of the McDonald home. This would serve them well in caring for Debbie after the accident.

There was never any doubt in anyone's mind that the McDonald home was a loving place and one where family was very important. Mac and Loraine were both raised as life-long Baptists. Their involvement at Clearwater Baptist Church was a central part of their life. Mac and Loraine's faith, nurtured as young people in the church of their parents and as a family at Clearwater Baptist, helped equip them to deal with the challenges they would face.

Debbie's Mom, Loraine

Loraine was the second child of Bill and Nora Wilson. The oldest child was Lockey, who was born in 1920. Loraine was born in 1922. The third child was Roy, who was born in 1925, and the fourth was Clint, who was born in 1932.

Bill was a strong man and an incredible baseball pitcher. In an editorial in the <u>Daily Post-Athenian</u>, the Athens, Tennessee hometown newspaper, the editor described how seeing big Bill Wilson pitch was one of his most memorable experiences growing up in Athens. This had occurred many years earlier in the editor's life. College eligibility rules were obviously looser in those days because Bill pitched for the Tennessee Wesleyan College baseball team, even though he did not attend the college. He also pitched in semi-pro ball for years until he injured his arm due to pitching too much and too often. I asked my mom once what she remembered about going to watch her dad pitch. Her reply was "He never lost." I laughed and replied to Mom, "Never." She looked at me and emphatically replied, "Never!" I can still remember pitching with my grandfather when I was growing up and being in awe of him.

For most of his working life, he was a machinist

for a copper mining company in Copperhill, Tennessee. This resulted in the family moving about from Athens, to Etowah and then to Copperhill before returning to Athens. For many years before Bill died of cancer in 1966, he would go to Copperhill to work during the week and then return to Athens on weekends.

Loraine's mother and my grandmother, Nora, was the prototypical matriarch. At one time, my two sisters and I, plus six of my cousins, lived on the same street with my grandmother. We, along with Butch and Debbie, would spend many hours at Mamaw's house. She kept most of the grandkids at some point while our parents worked. Since Papaw was away during the week, our strongest memories are of Mamaw living in a little two-bedroom house which was our second home. Time there included board games, swinging on the front porch, playing outside, and enjoying Mamaw's great cooking. Big meals like the Thanksgiving and Christmas lunches were a common occurrence at Mamaw's house.

The 12 cousins were all very close. Four of us, Butch, Jerry, Billy, and I were within a year of the same age. We spent tremendous amounts of time playing together. One of my uncles on the Toomey side of the family was driving his wife, who was pregnant with my cousin, Barbara; my mom, who was pregnant with me; Loraine, who was pregnant with Butch; and, Aunt Leona, who was pregnant with my cousin, Jerry, to the doctor. As he was driving, he said, "I hope we don't have an accident because I'm not sure how I'm going to explain why I'm in a car with four pregnant women." Our entire family was close because Loraine, her sister, Lockey, and her brothers, Roy and Clint, were very close.

Mamaw was the heart and glue and she was very dear to all of us.

Loraine was a beautiful and very bright young woman. If Loraine had been born in the last half of the 20th century, she would have attended college and could have pursued a variety of careers. However, growing up in the Great Depression, and having a father like Bill Wilson, meant getting an education was not to be her path. Loraine went to work at the age of 12 just like her sister, Lockey, had done. Their father believed that women did not need an education. Loraine ended up working until she married and had children. Loraine and Lockey both worked for Van Raalte hosiery mill where Lockey later became a supervisor.

Loraine worked and lived with her parents until she was 24. She had lots of friends and much of her time was spent enjoying those friendships and working with the youth at her church.

The nature and nurture question of human development is an interesting and perplexing one. Many people would argue vehemently that we are who we were born to be, and it is very difficult to overcome our basic DNA. Many identical-twin studies have been conducted where twins who were separated at birth for some reason are tracked in their adult years. They have discovered that these twins who are separated at birth often make very similar decisions and ended up living very similar lives despite being raised in very different environments.

At the same time, there is much support for the belief that we are shaped primarily by our environment. Behavioral psychology stresses the importance of the antecedents in our lives like role models, education and motivational goals. Behavioral psychology also puts a great deal of emphasis on the power of the consequences that come from our choices and actions in shaping our behavior. If the consequence is positive, we are more likely to make the same choice or exhibit the same behavior the next time in order to get the positive result. If the outcome is negative, then we are less likely to repeat that behavior because we don't want to get zapped again.

I believe the truth in relation to the "nature versus nurture debate" will not be known in this life. My belief is both nature and nurture are powerful influencers in our lives. Is my strong work ethic because it is in the Toomey/Wilson genes or because my mom and dad worked hard their entire lives? I don't think we will ever know whether it is a 50/50 contribution, 75/25 one way or the other, or some other mixture.

With this in mind, I believe Debbie was wired in a wonderful way when she came into this world. I also believe she had some incredible people in her life that provided very positive nurturing. I want to start with her mom, Loraine. Many of the following things could also be said of Mac.

Loraine was a bright, responsible, person of faith who was very devoted to family. Once she married and had children, her focus in life was being a wife, mother, and homemaker. I've always believed the best way to measure the effectiveness of a mother is to simply look at their children. I grew up with Butch and went to the same high school with him. He was an outstanding young man. He was kind, considerate, responsible, bright, and humble. He was liked by all who knew him and was a testimony to the quality of parenting he received. I mentioned earlier that some of the cousins felt Butch was a little overprotected. He never complained but acccpted those limitations and it certainly did not negatively affect the type of young man he became. Aunt Leona told me a story about Loraine letting Butch go hunting with the Wilson boys the fall before he died and how much he enjoyed it. After Butch's death, Loraine told Aunt Leona that she was so glad she let Butch go hunting.

Loraine's positive parenting with Debbie could be seen before the accident. She was a sweet little girl who loved her family and doing things with her Mom. This closeness they had went to a new level after the accident. Although Loraine's injuries prevented her from caring for Debbie in the immediate days after the accident, once Loraine recovered she never left her daughter's side. I'm sure there were times Loraine had to be away for things like a doctor's appointment but it seemed like she was always with Debbie. There was a total devotion to caring for her daughter that was fierce in its determination.

During Debbie's childhood years following the accident, the caregiving was physically, mentally and emotionally demanding. Loraine was there to help lift her from bed to chair. She prepared Debbie's meals, provided help with all of Debbie's personal needs, and helped Debbie find meaning in each and every day. That 24/7 type of commitment to the care of someone is probably one of the greatest acts of love on a human level. She was the primary one there to attend to Debbie's every need.

I asked Debbie one time where she learned the things she knew. Her response was that she learned everything she knew from God and her mom. I then asked her what were some of the most important things she had learned. The first thing she shared was that we learn from everything we do and experience. It was easy to see Debbie put that into practice and Loraine insured that she was able to continually learn new things.

The second thing she mentioned was that we should love everybody. Most of us struggle with that because it is so hard to love those who do harm to us or let us down in some way. I've never seen Debbie demonstrate dislike for anyone. She really seems to love everyone. This is what her family has seen for years but the staff at both caregiving facilities where Debbie has lived always point this out when you ask them to describe her. Her love is so genuine and makes it obvious Debbie learned this well from her mom.

The third thing Debbie learned from her mom was to honor and obey one's parents. This is coming from a conversation I had with Debbie when she was a 53 year-old adult. Because of Debbie's unique circumstances in life, dependency on her parents was certainly greater than those of us who experience more typical growing up years. As Debbie became older, she kept some of those precious child-like qualities. However, as she became more and more independent of her mom and dad when she moved to Sweetwater and then Woods Memorial Nursing Home, it became apparent that other than her necessary physical dependencies Debbie is a very capable adult. She has developed many wonderful relationships independently. She makes most of the decisions about her day-to-day functioning. In spite of this newfound independence, Debbie still recognizes that the commandment to honor and obey your parents involves a principle of respect for the ones who have invested the most into your life. Debbie has brought such honor to Loraine and Mac.

Certainly the family knows the sacrifices they've made and the labor of love they've given. Others like homebound teachers describe Loraine and Mac as wonderful parents. Debbie knows they earned her respect and she continues to give that. It is more about honor than obedience. Debbie learned that primarily from Loraine. That respect continues even though Loraine has passed away. Debbie honors her mom every morning. One of the nurses at Woods observed Debbie looking up and whispering one morning. When she asked Debbie what she was doing, Debbie told her that she talks to her mom every morning.

One of the most important things Debbie learned from God and her mom was the importance of trusting God and others and being trustworthy. Most of us believe that we should be honest and trustworthy, and we strive to do that. We all fail in that at times. Certainly, trustworthiness has never been an issue with Debbie. In fact one of the nurses, in describing Debbie, talked about how honest she is. She said "You always know what Debbie is thinking." Now, it is probably easy in Debbie's case because it seems her thoughts are almost always sweet, kind and positive. Trusting others is something many of us struggle with, and we put less emphasis on that. For Debbie, it is important to trust others. This makes a lot of sense because she has had to put her trust in others more so than most of us do. But a lot of the trust that Debbie places in others comes from her belief in the trustworthiness of others. It seems that this tends to bring out the best in people. Others seem to treat Debbie with the same kindness that she treats them.

One of the most important things Debbie has learned is how God protects us and we should, in turn, protect one another. Debbie might cite the following verses as one of the reasons she believes this about protection:

> *25 Therefore I say unto you, be not anxious for your life, what ye shall eat, or what ye shall drink; nor yet for your body, what ye shall put on. Is not the life more than the food, and the body than the raiment?*

> *26 Behold the birds of the heaven, that they sow not, neither do they reap, nor gather into barns; and your heavenly Father feedeth them. Are not ye of much more value then they?*

> *27 And which of you by being anxious can add one cubit unto the measure of his life?*

> *28 And why are ye anxious concerning raiment? Consider the lilies of the field, how they grow; they toil not, neither do they spin:*

> *29 yet I say unto you, that even Solomon in all his glory was not arrayed like one of these.*

> *30 But if God doth so clothe the grass of the field, which to-day is, and to-morrow is*

cast into the oven, shall he not much more clothe you, O ye of little faith?

31 Be not therefore anxious, saying, What shall we eat? or, What shall we drink? or, Wherewithal shall we be clothed?

32 For after all these things do the Gentiles seek; for your heavenly Father knoweth that ye have need of all these things.

33 But seek ye first his kingdom, and his righteousness; and all these things shall be added unto you. (Matthew 6: 25-33)

The meaning of these verses in brief is "do not worry." It does seem, to those who know Debbie, that she never worries. I believe she is able to do this because she trusts in God's protection and those who love her.

As a psychologist, I have counseled with about a thousand people and have encountered many who had struggles in their lives because they were "caretakers" and were "used" by others. Often their excessive protection of others was detrimental to those they were trying to protect because the person they were protecting never took responsibility for their destructive behavior. Earlier I mentioned that in our growing up years, some of us thought Loraine and Mac were overly protective of Butch and Debbie. My view has been that we can be too protective of people in a way that is not good for them.

After my conversation with Debbie, I thought a lot about my perspective on protection and the value

Debbie places on protecting one another. The more I thought about it the more I realized how important protecting others really is to me. I recalled how really important it was to protect my children, Kelly and Chris, when they were younger. I still want to protect them today even though they are very capable and independent young adults. However, when Kelly was battling breast cancer five years ago, I wanted to put this protective, healing shell around her. Protecting my wife is very important to me. As the husband, I take my role of insuring her safety very seriously. Do I hover over her? Definitely not - because she is a woman of strength and doesn't need my protection often, but there are times she does, and I want to be there for her as she is for me. As my mom approached death, she became so fragile and struggled with many things. A major focus in those days was protecting her from pain, discomfort, and fear.

I've concluded that Debbie is right. We need to look out for each other and consider when people around us are in need of protection. Loraine was the main human protector of Debbie. Mac, of course, and others helped with that, but Loraine was protector-in-charge and she served as a wonderful role model for Debbie in living out this lesson she had learned.

Our Pastor, Greg Depriest, had a beautiful sermon on the importance of caring for one another in a world that is sometimes very harsh and uncaring. He supported this with a story about Noah in Genesis 6. Noah, in the scriptures, is described as a just man, perfect amongst his generations, and a man who walked with God. This was why he was chosen to build the ark and save his family and the animals from the great flood. After the flood, Noah planted a vineyard and in a moment of weakness became drunk and was naked in his tent. In the midst of this unusual moment of weakness, Noah needed protection from his family who were spared from death because of his moral life and closeness to God. The first to discover Noah was his middle son, Ham. Instead of protecting his father from further embarrassment, he spread the word about this embarrassing situation to his two brothers Shem and Japheth. Fortunately, they responded with compassion. They took a garment and laid it on the back of their shoulders and backed into their father's tent and covered their father's nakedness.

Our world needs more of this type of compassion and caring for one another. Debbie learned this from her mother. When we experience challenges or problems, whether they are of our own making or chance, we need to protect each other from further pain, fear, embarrassment, or shame. Loraine covered Debbie with a love and protection that enabled her to face each day with hope.

The final lesson Debbie learned from Loraine was to be positive, look for the good, and never be discouraged. I'm sure this lesson was pounded out in the crucible of the life brought about as a result of the accident. Can you imagine what Debbie, Loraine, and Mac's life would have been like if they had not believed this or approached each day with this guiding them? We who were there could see this viewpoint in Loraine and Mac's life but not to the degree that it has been lived out through Debbie. This ability to approach life with positivity despite the constant physical challenges that life brought her way is the major thing that makes Debbie such an extraordinary individual. One of the main sources for this view toward life definitely came from Loraine.

Loraine was a key factor in this extraordinary life and she taught Debbie well.

Debbie's Dad, Mac

Many of the positive qualities and contributions Loraine made to Debbie's life apply to Mac also. Mac was not the constant presence because he worked to support the family so he was gone for 40 plus hours a week while Loraine was with Debbie practically all the time when they were in their home. Remember, every time I would ask Debbie questions like "what helped you the most in life?" the major response was God, Mom, and Dad. Mac and Loraine were the human partners in the trio that shaped Debbie's life. Loraine was the constant influence but Mac was equally important.

Austin McDonald, or Mac, was raised on a farm and was the son of a well-known Baptist minister in the area. Mac's father, C.E., was a major spiritual influence in a lot of people's lives including my father. My father was inspired to lead music in churches all those years because of the what he saw in the life of Rev. McDonald.

In the early years of Rev. McDonald's ministry, around 1930 at New Hopewell Baptist Church, a picture in the local newspaper showed 29 people waiting to be baptized in the waters of Mouse Creek, which was dammed to create a baptismal pool. In another local newspaper article entitled "Getting Dunked," a columnist by the name of Travis Wolfe told about being baptized by Rev. McDonald at North Cleveland Baptist Church. Mr. Wolfe said they called him Brother Mac and described him as a gentle, simple man and a preacher of the old-time religion. Mr. Wolfe was a gangly, 6-foot 7-inch 19-year old when he was preparing to be baptized by Rev. McDonald. Here's how he described the baptism:

"The top of Brother Mac's head came up to the middle of my chest and I felt apprehension as I stepped down into the water in the baptismal tank to be dunked. My hands shook. Brother Mac grinned. 'Don't worry', he said, taking hold of my arm. 'I'll get you under the water all right.' I gulped. That's not what I'm worried about. It's getting me back up – that worries me. He laughed, 'Nobody's drowned in a baptistery yet. Have you ever heard of anyone drowning in a baptistery?' Before I could answer no, Brother Mac grabbed hold of my nose, placed a flat hand on my spine and, with the other hand, pushed me backward into the water. I came up sputtering and, although I had barely gotten accustomed to the old one, I was ready to begin a new life."

In addition to being a pastor in churches his entire life, Rev. McDonald worked as a carpenter, mechanic, and at other jobs to provide for his family. This was important, because there were nine children in the family - five sisters and four brothers. Mac was the second oldest child. This provided a lot of hands on the farm which also helped in making a living. They had a few head of cattle, two mules, and a large garden.

Mac remembers spending most of his time outdoors enjoying the farm, hunting, and fishing. It was a good life growing up.

Mac, like my mom and dad and a lot of youth in 1930's, went to work when they could and did not finish high school. These were the days of the depression and so helping the family was necessary. Mac worked in a grocery store and developed a strong work ethic which served him well.

Mac's life changed significantly when he was called to military service in 1942. To understand the strength and determination of Mac, one should be aware of his experience in World War II in addition to his upbringing on a farm. Mac is like many brave veterans I've known. He is humble and never talked much about his military service, particularly his experiences in battle. In fact, Mac only talked about his WWII experience on one occasion with my father and Uncle Roy. The following description of Mac's military experience is taken from notes he wrote in preparation for an interview with a local newspaper. The newspaper was doing an article about him being a POW and getting the Purple Heart.

Mac was inducted into the Army on May 12, 1942 in Ft. Oglethorpe, GA. After a 10-day home leave to get his affairs in order, Mac went to Camp Wheeler, GA for basic training. From there, he went to Camp Kilmer, NJ to prepare for deployment overseas. He recalls being issued new clothing that was impregnated to protect the wearer from gas, and "boy did they stink." After about a week, they left out of New York on the Queen Elizabeth for Scotland.

His battalion was sent first to a location near Birmingham, England. There, they were given M1 rifles and trained for several days. After this training, they were taken to Scotland to board ships for a convoy going to Algiers, Africa. As they arrived, the Germans were bombing the harbor but none of their ships were hit.

In Algiers, Mac joined the 168th infantry and began rapid training. He then joined Company M which was a machine gun squad. They trained extensively with 30 caliber machine guns, heavy artillery, M1 rifles, 45 caliber pistols, grenades, and bayonets.

After several weeks, they boarded trucks and were sent to Tunisia arriving on the front at night. They dug in quickly with big guns all around them. The next morning, they began walking to higher ground. The tanks were going at it hot and heavy and German Stukas were dive bombing and Mac indicated the scream from those dives would "drive you crazy." The Stukas were two-man (pilot and rear gunner) dive bombers that specialized in ground-attacks. The tank battles were terrible, and many of the tanks were destroyed. Mac and his fellow infantry men were on a hill and the Germans were pouring it on them. When night came, they were left with only one way out and the order came to retreat.

They walked all night while carrying their guns and ammunition. When daylight came, the Germans were all around them. They were captured in Tunisia on February 17, 1943 as a part of the Rommel offensive. After a couple of early victories, the inexperienced troops were forced to retreat and many were captured during battles over a period of a month. A month later, General Patton, Field Marshall Montgomery, and the British troops began to reverse the tide of the war in Northern Africa.

The headline of the <u>Daily Post-Athenian</u> on March 9, 1943 read "Austin McDonald Missing In North Africa." The article then tells how a telegram received that morning from the War Department by Austin's mother indicated Mac had been missing since February 17, 1943. It then indicated it was reasonably assumed that Austin was in action during the Rommel push in the Tunisian area which began on February 17th and lasted for a few days. United States forces suffered substantial casualties in personnel and equipment in that fighting according to an announcement on February 18th by Secretary of War Stimson. A few days later news reports indicated that many Americans were taken prisoners in that action.

Official notification of Mac's captivity came to the McDonald family on July 8, 1943. In a telegram from the Adjutant General it said:

REPORT JUST RECEIVED THROUGH THE INTERNATIONAL RED CROSS STATES THAT YOUR SON PRIVATE AUSTIN E MCDONALD IS A PRISONER OF WAR OF THE GERMAN GOVERNMENT LETTER OF INFORMATION FOLLOWS.

The following was a response to a letter from Reverend McDonald inquiring about Mac's status:

Dear Reverend McDonald:

The Provost Marshal General directs me to reply to your letter of 16 August 1943, regarding your son, Private Austin E. McDonald. The records in this office indicate that your son is still interned at Dulag 226, Germany. No further information has been received concerning him since our letter of 10 July 1943. Information has been received which indicates that Dulag 226 is being used as a semi-permanent camp. It is for this reason that parcel labels will be forwarded on or about 11 September 1943, for his benefit. Please be assured that you will be informed immediately when further information is received regarding you son.

Sincerely yours,

Assistant Director

Prisoner of War Division

After they were captured, the first food they received was one can of sardines and a slice of black bread. They then went to Tunis where they were loaded on cargo planes and flown to the town of Reggio, Italy, which was across from Sicily.

U.S planes were bombing the airfield on one end as they landed which made it necessary for them to jump out of the plane and run for shelter. The POW's were taken to a remote place on the edge of town where they put up tents with straw on the ground and were forced to sleep side by side.

The captured soldiers were given a slice of black German bread with jelly for breakfast, a cup of water soup with bread for lunch, and something the German captors called coffee with both meals. They soon had body lice and bad cases of diarrhea, and were not allowed to take baths.

Their days involved working in ammunition dumps, digging air raid shelters, and unloading box cars in rail yards, while frequently being bombed. They also worked in food warehouses, docks with ships going to Sicily, gasoline dumps, and they cleaned up after air raids.

Americans bombed by day and the English by night. One night their camp was bombed with fire bombs and one hit their camp stove.

Mac had a painful tooth that was removed in Reggio. The Italians were friendly at first but when the bombing intensified, the locals called them everything under the sun and threw rocks at them. One lady threw her shoes.

After about four months and twenty days in Reggio, the Allies were bombing Sicily night and day. This bunch of starved, dirty and sick soldiers were hungry for some good news. Good news came when a group of new guards arrived from Germany with Red Cross parcels. There was one box for every two men. The guards indicated that they were signed up for Red Cross and would be taken to Germany. They were loaded up onto two box cars on July 12, 1943. The Italian box cars were small and designed for 40 men, and it was very crowded.

The train was going up the coast and about noon an air raid began on the train. The engineer stopped the train and ran off. The first planes blew the train doors off and "we got out and ran for safety." As Mac dived behind a stone wall, he was hit in the hip and it began bleeding profusely. Several were killed, and Mac's best friend experienced injuries that resulted in his feet swelling up so badly that he could not wear shoes.

A few hours after this attack, they were loaded onto another box car and taken to a large camp near Naples. The Americans were on one side and the English were on the other. While at this camp, Mac received treatment for his hip wound which included shots for four days. Around the first of August of 1943, they left this camp for a Russian camp in Hammerstein, Germany and arrived there around August 6. This was a cold, dirty, and dismal place. It had been very hot when they left Italy and the GIs had cut off their pants to make them like shorts and did not have many clothes. Before they could go into the old barracks, they were required to take baths and have all their clothes deloused. The POW's were given wooden shoes, French coats, Russian pants, one blanket, and a straw mattress. They received very little rations.

Mac and his fellow prisoners were not there very long before their German captors started sending them to work on farms and at other camps. On August 18, 1943, eleven of them were sent to a large farm called Kessburg. It was owned by an elderly lady and her daughter and run by a manager. There were lots of French soldiers and Russian civilians serving as labor. Mac and the other prisoners were put in a small stone house with a high wire fence and the gate and the house were locked at night. Four Russian soldiers were already living in the house. The new arrivals were used for putting bundles of grain into shocks to dry for the threshing machine; picking potatoes, carrots, and sugar beets; digging ditches and hauling dirt; and, cleaning manure out of stalls and barns. They were basically farm hands doing any type of farm work.

Health issues were a major problem. Mac had more teeth pulled and the only way he could treat the pain was by chewing tobacco. He had an infected finger that almost never healed.

After a few months, the Germans sent the Russian soldiers away and brought in more Americans. The Germans worked them long and hard. One of Mac's fellow GIs was from New York and became the cook. They would combine the meat from their Red Cross boxes and make stew. The Germans gave them plenty of potatoes and a little milk but very little meat.

After over a year on the farm in Keesburg, everyone knew the Russian guns were getting louder and so the decision was made to move Mac and the other American prisoners. It was January of 1945 and it was very cold and the snow was deep. They had to carry their own food and all their clothes on their backs. They walked in the daytime and slept in pig stalls, cow barns, sheep sheds, and horse stalls. Mac had his 26th birthday resting in an old barn full of straw.

While on this march, Mac had to carry heavy loads of supplies on his back. He developed boils on his neck that would burst over and over because they were not allowed to heal due to the dirty conditions.

Boiled potatoes were about the only thing they were given to eat. Mac remembers getting a piece of horse meat once, and one day a boy gave him a big swig of Russian whiskey which kept him warm all day. It was a relief to get out of the snow. They walked most of each day, and he recalls walking at times on the Autobahn.

They encountered many civilians trying to get away from the Russians also. After a while, the soldiers would put them to work along the way. One day while digging a ditch, they learned that President Roosevelt was dead. Many of the prisoners of war had never heard of Truman when they learned he was now their President. When Mac was captured in late 1942, President Truman had been a little known Senator from Missouri. He was a compromise Vice-Presidential candidate who became President after being the Vice-President for only 82 days.

They began a cycle of working until the guns got closer and then moving to a new location. Their work was setting out pines, which was hard, but their hope and excitement was building because they had discovered the Americans were coming and the Russians were getting closer.

On May 2, 1945, they were liberated by the U.S. troops. Shortly after the troops moved on, and they were on their own for a few days. Mac recalls a chaplain coming to check on them. He also recalled a lot of singing and celebrating. The local Athens paper even ran an article about Mac being liberated.

The process of gathering up the prisoners of war and getting them on the road back home began. They rode on trucks through Germany into Alsace-Lorraine and then on to France. Once there, Mac and the other prisoners were taken to Camp Lucky Strike near Le Havre, France. Le Havre is situated in the north-western part of the country, at the mouth of the river Seine on the English Channel. Camp Lucky Strike was a staging area for troops. The camps like these were named after cigarettes for security reasons to protect their locations.

Mac and his fellow soldiers were fattened up with great food and egg nog and ate all they could. From the camp, they boarded ships and began their trip home from the Le Havre harbor. Mac's status was communicated to his family in the following telegram from the Adjutant General on June 19, 1945:

8:03 AM: THE CHIEF OF STAFF OF THE ARMY DIRECTS ME TO INFORM YOU YOUR SON PVT MCDONALD AUSTIN E IS BEING RETURNED TO THE UNITED STATES WITHIN THE NEAR FUTURE AND WILL BE GIVEN AN OPPORTUNITY TO COMMUNICATE WITH YOU.

Mac did not wait long before he sent this telegram to his family a little over 5½ hours later:

1:45 PM: BACK IN STATES FEELING FINE FURLOUGH SOON WILL WRITE NEXT STATION. LOVE= MAC

Mac was a prisoner of war from February 17, 1943 to May 8, 1945. The last fighting of American troops occurred on May 6, 1945. The journey back to the states for Mac ended at Camp Patrick Henry in Newport, Virginia. Ironically, Camp Patrick Henry also served as a prisoner of war camp, housing over 5,000 German prisoners of war during 1944 and 1945. The prisoners worked there to alleviate the critical shortage of manpower in the area. This was done within the limits of the Geneva Convention. To show how different these German prisoner of war experiences were to Mac and his fellow POWs, Camp Patrick Henry had a prisoner-of-war canteen within the compound where the prisoners, within existing regulations, could make limited purchases.

To take this irony to another level, the first German prisoners-of-war to be permanently assigned to this camp were members of the Africa Corps who had been captured in the early part of 1943 in North Africa. So in a matter of months after Mac was captured in North Africa and began his journey through Italy, Germany, France, and now to Camp Patrick Henry, these German prisoners were captured in North Africa and ended up at the same camp.

From Camp Patrick Henry, Mac and his fellow POWs were sent home for a one-month furlough. After the furlough, they were sent to Miami, FL for a thorough check-up and rehabilitation. While staying in the best hotels, their food was still C-Rations, individually canned, pre-cooked and prepared wet ration food. Mac was still in the military and he and his fellow soldiers helped clean up after a hurricane that hit the area where they were located.

Mac had to make a decision about whether to stay in the military. This was not an easy decision, and in some ways he believed he should stay. However, he felt he had served his country and wanted to go back to civilian life.

Mac indeed served his country well. The Purple Heart is a United States medal awarded in the name of the President to members of our military who have been wounded or killed while serving our country. As a recipient of the Purple Heart and a missing in action prisoner of war, he demonstrated the courage, determination, and resourcefulness that would enable him to help Debbie face the tremendous challenges she would face.

Mac has handled the adversity in his life with the same fortitude and bravery he demonstrated in his POW experience. He also responded to adversity with the same quiet strength, gratitude, and humility with which he approached everything. The determination we see in Debbie is the same resolve to move ahead that is evident in Mac's life.

Commitment to family is a major value for both the McDonalds and the Wilsons. This of course could be seen in Mac and Loraine's devotion in caring for Debbie. There is evidence of the strength of those family bonds in the letters written between Mac and his family during his POW experience. The following are some of those letters or excerpts from them.

I am sequencing these chronologically. Remember that Mac became a POW on February 17, 1943 and was liberated May 8, 1945. For some of

Mac's letters from Germany, I've included descriptions of the significant events in the war that occurred on the day or days Mac was writing in order to provide some context to the letters.

Letter from Mac's sister, Wanda, on Jan. 6, 1943:

Dear Austin,

I will try and write you a few lines tonight as I'm thinking about my big brother and wondering if you are alright. Haven't heard from you in so long that we don't know what to think. The last letter we got was after you had arrived in North Africa. You sure have traveled since you left the states haven't you? Austin have you ever gotten any of our mail? Sure hope you have. But if you haven't, don't think that we have forgotten you, for we sure haven't. Who could forget such a good brother as you? But we write to you every week.

What did you do on Christmas Day? We had a very good time. All our thoughts were of you. So you see you still are remembered by the rest of the McDonalds.

Everything is alright around here I guess. Not any new things happening. We're still having some good services at Clearwater. And we still remember our soldier boys.

I saw Polly in town the other Saturday. She was asking all about you. Said she hadn't heard from you yet. Did you ever get the Christmas boxes that she and we sent you?

We sure have been having some cold weather here. But it looks like rain tonight.

Mother and Dad are well and still praying for their Big Boy and for his safe return home out in the future.

I will close. Hoping to hear from you very soon.

Love,

Wanda

Letter from Mac's mother on Jan. 8, 1943 before he was captured:

Dear Austin,

Here I come again this snowy morning in January. It looks like it is going to be a big snow. Is it warm where you are? I sure hope so for it would be terrible to know you were suffering with cold along with everything else.

Everything is O.K. here the children are going to school and making pretty good grades. And the rest of us stay here and try to keep the home fires burning.

Austin what did you do Christmas day? I hope you got all the letters we have been sending you and read letters all day long for it would have taken most that long to have read all we have sent you and the ones all your friends have written too.

I can't understand why you can't get mail for we have sent you V.Mails and just common letters and Daddy registered you one and he has never had any returns from it and it has been about a month since he sent it. He has sent you some letters I sure do wish you could have gotten.

Vancil and R.C. have moved to Late Kennedy's farm and are milking cows they like very well.

Austin you ought to see Wade and his calves. They are great big things now but he sure can handle them. We have our mules at home now and we just have to watch him to keep him away from them. Charles and Billy sure believe in having fat stock for they double feed them sometimes. Joyce is growing and getting so tall you would hardly know her I bet. She still talks fast just like she used to and thinks she is flying. She gets letters from a boy in Braggs, Oklahoma. Robert told him about her and they have written several letters.

Wanda and Freda went to prayer meeting with their fellows last night but they say none of them can come up with their big soldier brother.

Daddy is getting along pretty well at North Athens Baptist Church. He went down to Cleveland Christmas day and preached and got to see Preacher Lewis again. And I sit at home looking out the window and wishing for my boy to come home. Oh how I wish for this terrible war to get over so all you boys could come home but there isn't a thing we can do about it but wish, hope, and pray that it will soon be over.

Buddy you tell us not to worry but we can't help it. If we could hear from you more often it would not be so bad but we haven't heard from you in a month and that is a long time to wait. I wish you would send us another cablegram for they come so much quicker.

So hoping and praying that we will all be together soon. I will close.

Lots of love,

Your Mother

P.S. Preacher Brown (Associational Missionary) has written you lots of letters. Do you get them?

As I mentioned earlier, Mac is a man of few words. The following notes are letters he wrote while he was a POW:

June 4, 1944:

It is Sunday again and I can forget for a little while this lonely existence in exile. Fond memories make themselves more predominant on Sunday. And we all look forward to the one day we don't work. (On June 5, Rome fell to the Allies, becoming the first capital of an Axis nation to do so.)

June 25, 1944:

Dearest Folks, I'm wondering what you are doing today? Going to different places I guess. I think if I was back there I would just stay at home. Hope all are well. I am still O.K. and working. Nothing new here. Write often. Love, Mac (On June 26, Cherbourg is liberated by American troops.)

On July 4, 1944:

Dear Folks, Just a line to let you know I am OK. Hope all are fine. I am still working hard. So much I'd like to talk to you about but must wait awhile. Write often. I usually get a letter a week. Love Mac (Our Independence Day)

September 10, 1944:

Mom, you had better get some strong apron strings for I want you to tie me to them when I get back (ha). (On September 10: Luxembourg is liberated by U.S. First Army; two Allied forces meet at Dijon, cutting France in half; first Allied troops enter Germany, entering Aachen, a city on the border.)

Oct 22, 1944:

Dearest Folks, Last week I was made happy. I received mail from home. The first for quite a while. Just keep them coming. They sure are welcome. I am still at the same place. We have fifty four guys here now. But none from around home. Atlanta GA is about the closest. Say, why don't you send me some pictures? I'll bet you all have changed a lot. Wade, are you as big as I am? I'll bet you are.

I don't hear from Polly (his girlfriend). Two letters since I left the states. I guess she didn't think so much of me after all (ha).

In a later letter Mac writes, "I was disappointed to hear about Polly, but after two years, what could you expect?" (October 21:

Aachen is occupied by U.S. First Army; it is the first major German city to be captured.)

December 3, 1944:

To his brothers and sisters - "All you boys and girls remember that I think of you every day."

December 10, 1944:

After almost two years in captivity, Mac wrote to his family:

Dear Homefolks,

Just fifteen days until Christmas. Here's hoping you have a pleasant time. My shopping will be sorta small this year I suppose. Hope all are well. I am still OK. Love to All, Mac (On December 8: The softening up bombardment of Iwo Jima begins.)

In all of Mac's brief notes to the family he always hoped his family was well; let them know he was working hard; and, told them he was OK. Just like Debbie, he was basically saying "I'm fine." At times the expected loneliness and weariness would show, but that was never the major focus. It was always about letting the family know how much he loved and missed them and reassuring them that he was "fine" in the midst of this terrible situation.

In this letter from Mac's father you can see the concern about his son after two years of captivity. You can also see his faith that Mac would be alright.

Letter from Mac's father on Feb. 1, 1945

Dear Austin,

How are you today? We are well and fine I guess. The boys are making so much racket I can hardly write and Grandpa Mac is here now. It is pretty but cold today.

Austin, we have had some fine letters from you and it does me so much good to know you are alright and able to work. It is also good to know you are still trusting the Lord for I believe He will help you to come home soon. So, keep on keeping on for the Lord for without Him we don't have much.

Austin, have you been injured in any way? I hope not. It seems like you can tell us so little about yourself. Tell us all you can about yourself and your surroundings and friends. Austin, we all like our home fine and have lots to do yet. Yes Mr. and Mrs. Wattenbarger said for you to hurry home for they need you. Everyone is asking about you. I sure will be a proud Dad when you get home and be able to tell people the Lord will hear prayers and go around with you. Boy won't that be grand.

Well I am going to town after the girls for they get off at noon. I sure was glad you got to go to church. Austin, do you stay in a camp or out on the farm?

Keep faith,

Dad

Finally, Mac was able to write the note home that the family had been looking for.

Dear Dad, Mom, and All,

I am hoping that everyone is well at home. As for me, I am fine. Was liberated the second day of May. I am now in France, in a rest camp. Awaiting my time to return home.

We are getting plenty of good G.I. food and boy, do we eat. No one can know what it means to a guy to be free again. And when I can get back to the good old U.S.A. and better still, on back home, to you, my happiness will be complete.

Hoping to see you soon.

Love

Mac

Mac faced numerous trials and tribulations as a soldier. These included: being separated from loved ones for over two years; facing death; being wounded by artillery fire; and, facing hunger and captivity.

These challenges revealed his strength of character and probably developed further qualities like courage, determination, persistence of hope, and an abiding faith in God. These qualities would serve him well as he faced Butch's death and Debbie's injuries. He carried the resolve of that POW soldier with a Purple Heart into his role as a father in that challenging situation.

That resolve was there in the simple way Mac would come home for lunch everyday to help. Debbie's mobility was so limited that moving from place to place was very difficult, and Mac was the one who did the heavy physical lifting.

Mac provided for the family financially, and the family never wanted. The financial burden of providing for the special needs of Debbie was significant, I'm sure, and Debbie received excellent medical care.

One of the major qualities about Debbie is her ability to focus on the moment and not regret the past or fear the future. I believe a lot of this comes from Mac and his life experience as a farmer, which is a defining role in Mac's life. He was raised on a farm, used his skills as a farmer to survive as a POW, worked a farm until the accident, and then gardened all the years he lived next to us on Jones Street. By the way, his garden was always the envy of my dad. Farmers know you have to take things a day at a time. You can't plant until you've prepared the ground. You can't expect the seed to grow unless the ground has nutrients, sun, moisture and a weed-free environment. You can't harvest the fruit of the vine until it is fully developed. You do what you need to each day and you can't change the lack of rain yesterday and you can't make the sun shine tomorrow. I believe Debbie's ability to live in the moment was influenced to a significant degree by the way she saw her father live his own life.

I once asked Mac how Debbie had affected his life. He said that first of all, she taught him how to love more. Mac certainly loves Debbie, and it is evident in the devotion he shows to her and her care. His face brightens up with a big smile every time he talks about Debbie. The second way she impacted him was she brought him out of his shell. My Uncle Mac is a quiet man who loved the solitude of his farming. He is always very friendly but shares little about himself. Debbie helped him open up through the years. Many of the challenges Debbie faced required Mac to go into situations outside his comfort zone. His willingness do things that were not easy for him to make things better for Debbie said more about his love for her than words could ever say - a father's love for his daughter.

Aunt Lockey

As I considered writing Debbie's story, I wanted to tell it with a total focus on her incredible life. I knew it would be impossible to tell it without looking at the central role that Loraine and Mac played and also the role of the rest of her family. However, I also knew that for the 51 years that Debbie lived while my mom was living the two of them had a special relationship. Mom was the one that was by Debbie's side the most in the month following the accident.

Debbie and her family lived next door to Mom for 40 years and she was a constant source of help during those years.

I did not want a son's love and respect to affect the way I described my mother's role in this story. As I began collecting information for the book, I even strove to err on the side of minimizing Mom's role in Debbie's life. The week before I began writing I sat down with Mac and asked him some questions. One of the questions I asked was "What helped you and Loraine deal with the challenges you faced?" Mac's first response was "We could not have made it without Lockey." I consciously did not pursue that at the moment and just asked him what else helped.

We finished talking and I walked down the hall from his room at the assisted living facility where he is now living. As I walked, I wanted to know more about why Mac felt they could not have made it without Mom. I then realized that if I wanted to tell Debbie's story accurately I had to address openly Mom's role. I turned around and went back to Mac's room.

When Mac came to the door, I told him that I wanted to ask him about something he had said. I asked him how Mom had helped them. I will never forget his response. Tears came to his eyes and with more animation than was normal for Mac he responded: "Wow, in every way: physically, mentally, emotionally, and spiritually. She took us to places we would have never gone." Tears then came to my eyes because this confirmed to me the role Mom had played in Debbie, Lorraine, and Mac's lives. I knew the love, passion, and commitment she poured into their lives and to have that confirmed by Mac was an affirmation that I sensed Mom was hearing also.

To give you a sense of why this lady was so instrumental in their lives, I want to share a story about my mom. When Mom had her last heart attack and surgery to clear two arteries and insert a stent, we were told she probably would not survive the surgery. As Marcie, Chris, my son, and I sat nervously in the waiting room, we cried together thinking we would never see Mom alive again. After about an hour, a young, exceptional heart surgeon came bouncing through the door with a big smile on his face and the first words out of his mouth were "Boy, she's a tough cookie!" Knowing my Mom, we were not surprised. He proceeded to tell us about the difficulty of the surgery and how they had to restart Mom's heart four times. He went on to tell us how she was doing and then smiled and said, "Your mom is so sweet." He then shared with us that at one point in the surgery, he walked by Mom's head and was feeling a little frustrated. At this point Mom was awake and looked up at him and said, "You're having a rough day aren't you." One of the nurses later told us that most patients are either scared or complaining during surgery but Mom was showing concern for them instead.

Mom was a tough cookie and the rock of our family. She was strong enough to drop out of school when she was 12 and work 13 hours a day seven days a week to help her family during the Great Depression. She was strong enough to raise three kids, work a 40-hour week, teach Sunday School, sing in the choir, cook, and keep up a home for her family. She was strong enough to supervise 50 ladies in a hosiery mill. She was strong enough to care for her family in the toughest moments whether it was her father's death with cancer, Debbie's recovery from traumatic injuries, Dad's illnesses and death, my sister's bout with cancer and death, or any of the other family challenges. She lost both parents, her husband, a daughter, two younger siblings, and other family members, and she always found strength from her heavenly Father. God was that source of strength, but with Mom, God had some good material with which to work.

My mother is also one of the most giving human beings I've ever known. One of the most frustrating things about my mom was she always was so busy doing for others that you could never get her to do something for herself. She was the consummate caretaker. My sisters and I benefited greatly from that care giving whether it was the clothes she made, the meals she cooked, or the support she offered during all the trials of life. At times, as we grew into adulthood, it was a little frustrating because Mom had a hard time turning off that care giving mode.

Debbie provided a great outlet for Mom's nurturing behavior. Mom would tell people that Debbie was her adopted daughter even though Debbie already had two wonderful parents. Mom took her relationship with Debbie seriously, and everyone knew it was a priority in her life. Dad, my sisters, and I found great joy in the commitment she had to Debbie's care. We knew how much help Mom was to Debbie, Loraine, and Mac and we knew how much joy and satisfaction Mom received in being there for them.

This special place in Debbie's life began when Mom went to stay in the hospital with Debbie after the accident. Earlier, I shared some words from Becky Wooden, who was one of Debbie's nurses, about what those days were like. Now I want to share Becky's thoughts and feelings about Mom.

> "As I look back over my life, this experience with this wonderful family ranks high on the list of my most memorable experiences. Not only do I have the joy of knowing that God used me and allowed me to play a small role in the life of this precious child at a time when her life hung in the balance, I also have the added bonus of a life-long friendship with one of the Godliest ladies I've ever known – her Aunt Lockey. We both know that our loving Heavenly Father arranged for us to have that special time with each other and with Debbie after so many years – it certainly qualifies as one of life's extras."

Mom was a critical part of the support for Debbie during those early days. I believe she brought a determination to fight the dim prognosis. She refused to accept a bad outcome. I'm convinced her prayers, her talking to and touching Debbie even though she could not respond outwardly, and her always looking for ways to make things better helped Debbie live and get to the point that she could function at a high level considering her injuries.

The relationship which began in the hospital continued after Debbie came home. Mom saw Debbie every day. It was usually multiple times and for hours not minutes. Mom was there to help with the small tasks, to provide encouragement during the many tough times, and to work at making things better each day.

As Debbie moved toward and into her adult years, Mom's biggest contribution was described very succinctly when Mac said, "She took us to places we would have never gone." Mac was not speaking only of physically going to places they would have never gone even though that was true. Mom was always encouraging them to go together out to eat, go on a picnic, or go sightseeing and gradually these activities became a regular part of their lives. They were quite a foursome.

The family also went to places they would have never gone in terms of stretching the limits of what Debbie was capable of doing socially, mentally, and in other ways. Mom believed in Debbie and her capabilities. She focused more on what Debbie could do than what she could not do. After Mom came to live with us, she continued to consider how to make the quality of Debbie's life better. Mom never accepted the status quo. She always wanted to help make things better. She would share her ideas with me. I in turn would listen to her talk with Debbie on the phone and watch her when we visited share thoughts about things Debbie could do.

Mom and Debbie had a special bond. It was grounded in a deep love for one another and similar viewpoint. Both of them tackled whatever life presented them with a belief that something good could be produced. That optimism and fortitude was a critical part of that bond. I think Debbie learned a lot of that from my mom.

As much as Mom gave, she probably received even more in return. Loraine and Mac were always so appreciative of everything she did. However, what made it all worthwhile was the relationship with Debbie. It brought such joy and fulfillment. Debbie is special and the love she gave my Mom was special.

Family

The burden of care that Loraine and Mac carried with considerable help from my mom was incredible and they carried the brunt of that load. However, their families provided a great deal of support. Both the Wilsons and McDonalds played and continue to play an important role.

During the early years following the accident, my observations were primarily from the perspective of the Wilson family. Immediately after the accident, Loraine, Mac and Debbie moved in with Mamaw Wilson who lived down the street from us. They lived in another house between Mamaw's and our house. About a year after the accident, they moved into the house next door to us. As a result, I was able to observe the involvement of Loraine's family very closely, whether it was Mamaw, Loraine's siblings and their spouses, or cousins and their spouses over the years.

Mamaw was such an important part of those early years. Mamaw was 65-years old when the accident occurred. Even at this point in her life she was a small and frail lady. She helped in small ways physically, but as the matriarch of our family all twelve cousins competed for her attention. We loved staying with her and she seemed to love having us around. Seeing Debbie daily was an important part of her day, and if you were at her house, you went with her. Debbie loved the family get-togethers at Mamaw's and this social interaction with the family help lay the foundation for Debbie moving so effortlessly into the residential settings that became her homes. Other than her mom, dad and her aunt Lockey, Mamaw is the other person Debbie specifically mentioned as helping her deal with the challenges in her life.

Loraine's brother, Roy, and his wife Leona, were there often and provided tremendous physical and moral support. The other brother Clint and his wife, Edna, did the same until they relocated to Greeneville, S.C. The cousins assisted in some physical ways like helping Debbie with physical therapy, but the most important role was visiting and insuring Debbie knew she was loved and was an important part of the family. This included playing games, catching up on what everyone was doing, and joking with each other. We knew each other first as kids, and those playful shared times have never ceased. These fun loving relationships are very similar to the type of relationships Debbie is able to build with the staff that cares for her and her fellow residents.

I know from things Debbie has shared with me that she has the same type of relationship with members of her father's family. The members of both families have a very special place in their hearts for Debbie.

Two family members who have been an essential part of Debbie's life, especially over the last ten years are Mac's youngest brother, Bill, and his wife, Dixie. As Mom moved into her 80's, she was increasingly limited in the things she was able to do with and for Debbie. She saw Debbie everyday until she came to live with us in 2007, but she was unable to carry a heavy physical load. Bill and Dixie filled that void. They became the chief support for the family. They helped them make the move to the assisted living facility. They helped Loraine deal with several hospitalizations and moves from one facility to another. They helped with the eventual move for both Debbie and Loraine to Woods. At the same time, Mac returned home for a brief period before settling into another assisted living facility closer to Debbie.

Bill and Dixie were and still are indispensable. The wonderful thing is the way they help out of love and not obligation. Bill and Debbie are always joking with each other, and it is easy to see the love Debbie has for both of them. Mom's biggest worry during her last years was what would happen to Debbie after Loraine and Mac were no longer here or able to care for Debbie. The rest of the family shared that concern. We all appreciated and admired the way Bill and Dixie managed the tough issues and situations that led to Debbie finding a home at Woods. It gave us great peace of mind. We could see that Debbie had found a wonderful caring home and was very happy.

Earlier I referenced a dream my Mom had a week before she died. Let me tell the full story. On that morning Mom woke up and immediately told me she wanted to share something she had dreamed that night. I went to get my wife, Marcie, and sister,

Carolyn, and we all sat down in front of Mom. She told us that she dreamed Jesus was standing in front of her with His arms outstretched, and she didn't know what to do. When we approach death, it is important for the people we love to give us permission to die. If we don't get that permission, we often hang on and suffer in the process. I took Mom's hands and said to her: "Mom, your work here is done. We will all miss you when you leave this earth but we are all O.K. Carolyn's O.K. I'm O.K. and all of your grandchildren and great grandchildren are O.K. And, Debbie's O.K. You will always be a wonderful part of us but we will all be fine. So, the next time you see Jesus with His arms outstretched, you run into those arms. That's what we all want for you."

I could not have given that assurance to Mom without the things that Bill and Dixie did to help Debbie find a good earthly home. We will always be thankful for all they have done.

When I talked with Debbie before beginning to write this, she was talking about family and she said; "A family is like a team and good teamwork is a key to making things good for everyone." The Wilsons and McDonalds have been a good team and that made it better for everyone, especially Debbie. It has been such a joy to be a part of the Debbie team.

Debbie

Even when one considers the positive influence

of Loraine, Mac, her aunt Lockey, and the rest of the family, from my perspective, the way Debbie responds to her life circumstances is still incredible. We all have the potential to respond in such a positive, determined, and courageous way, but most of us probably would not.

I believe there is something very special about Debbie. This uniqueness is a combination of intelligence, character, strength of will, and world-view.

Debbie's intelligence is obvious in the way her mind is like a steel trap that remembers facts, names, and situations that the vast majority of us would forget. She also shows her intelligence with her quick wit. Her sense of humor is creative and informed by her intelligence. She faces every learning challenge and is able to grasp whatever she needs to know to adapt to very challenging circumstances.

A popular concept in the business world these days is "emotional intelligence." I believe Debbie is a genius in this area. Consider the challenge of living in a sheltered environment for 45 years and then being thrown into a world of many new people including caregivers and residents representing a wide range of ages. Debbie not only handled those situations, she thrives in them. In spite of her speech and other physical limitations, Debbie has incredible interpersonal skills. As the staff members at Woods say, everyone loves Debbie. She loves being with people and they love being with her.

Debbie's determination is truly unique. As family members helped her with her rehab, we agonized as we did it. Debbie pushed on through despite the pain. Just getting up and going everyday is a challenge that requires a type of determination that I'm seldom called upon to exhibit. The people who know Debbie emphasize they never hear her complain about her lot in life. She confronts each situation with a positive can-do attitude be it: countless surgeries and other medical setbacks; change in surroundings that are outside her control; or, the loss of loved ones. I asked Debbie if there was anything she would change about her life, and she said "No." I find this an amazing response. Debbie does not live in the past or the future. She resides in the moment and believes that each moment has wonderful possibilities. To focus on the past and wish things had been different is a waste of energy for Debbie. There are too many good things to be celebrated in the moment. Debbie does not waste time dreaming about the future because I believe she recognizes that the future really does not promise or assure us of anything on this earth. Debbie tackles things one day at a time with an abiding faith that provides her with the confidence that things will work out for good.

Debbie's positive attitude is amazing. During the Baltimore Ravens run to winning the Super Bowl in 2013, Coach John Harbaugh heard about a young man named Matthew Jeffers who had dealt with physical limitations his entire life. He came to speak to the Ravens and one of the things he told the team was that the only disability in life is a bad attitude. Based on this comment, Debbie has no disabilities. Her attitude is the most positive I have ever seen. It is not a trumped up surface optimism. It is not simply something seen in a particular situation. It is deep, enduring, and positive, and it dictates her response to every situation. She simply dives into everything with a genuine belief that a good outcome is possible.

The last thing I did to get more information for this book was to look through some things that Mac had stored after he sold their house on Jones Street. In a storage chest I found the book Power of Positive Thinking by Norman Vincent Peale. I had read this book many years ago. The book has a scripture, some thoughts by Rev. Peale, and a prayer for each day of the year. If anyone has a positive attitude, it is Debbie and so I looked for key thoughts from this book that might have influenced her. I picked special days of the year for Debbie, like birthdays of special people in her life and other special occasions. As I reviewed the writings of Rev. Peale, it was amazing how the positive thoughts from this popular book are so evident in Debbie's life. Debbie and her parents insured that her life was surrounded by positive people and positive ideas.

In Kurt Goldstein's book, The Organism: A Holistic Approach to Biology Derived from Pathological Data in Man, he proposes a theory that all organisms have a tendency to actualize themselves or bring themselves into being. Abraham Maslow expanded this concept to human motivation by proposing that people are motivated by a hierarchy of needs. Maslow's theory said that once human beings meet the lower level needs of basic physical needs, safety and security, belonging, and status, they are motivated by the highest level need of self-actualization. In other words, the highest level motivation in life is to realize our full potential. Many of us probably never get there.

I believe Debbie is a self-actualized person. She,

within her physical limitations, has reached her full potential. Self-actualized persons have a proper sense of self. They are humble yet they are confident in their strengths and what they are capable of accomplishing. A humorous illustration of Debbie's sense of self is a common interaction she has with her father. Almost every time Mac visits Debbie at the nursing home, he asks "Debbie, do you think you and I will ever amount to anything?" Debbie without hesitation responds every time with "Well I already have." Debbie knows who she is and is totally at peace with that. I recently heard a song entitled "If I Give It All" and written by Will Reagan. The song shares how when we put our lives in God's hands He makes something beautiful out of us. God truly made something beautiful out of Debbie McDonald.

A good illustration of this confidence Debbie has as result of resting in God's hands is her response to my mother's death. When Mom died, my sister and I began calling all the family to let them know and share with them the funeral arrangements. When I called Debbie, I knew she would respond with grace and hope. She was so close to Mom and I knew she would rejoice that Mom was with her heavenly Father. I also knew that Debbie had never been to a funeral but I wanted Debbie to know that we would love for her to share in the memorial service. She indicated she would be there.

Can you imagine what it would be like to go to a funeral service for the first time at age 52 after living in a sheltered environment? Debbie arrived about 30 minutes before the service and we were in the process of receiving friends. Dixie rolled Debbie down the aisle and nervously handed Debbie over to me. We were all a little concerned about how Debbie would deal with this new situation. What a waste of our time and energy. Debbie goes into every situation with a sense of confidence and purpose. She can be confident because she is always relying on God's strength and guidance which is always sufficient. Her purpose was to celebrate and pay respects to a woman she loved and who had meant so much to her. There was no reason, from Debbie's perspective, to be nervous. Debbie and I began to visit with family and friends and she brought a smile to everyone's face.

When the memorial service began, I asked Marcie to sit with Debbie at the front of the chapel so Debbie could see everything. I would occasionally look over at Debbie and she always had a smile as we sang songs that Mom loved and as my son shared a message about God's working in Mom's life. I will also never forget hearing her voice above everyone else as we sang Amazing Grace. Debbie comprehends the significance of the moment as much as anyone I've ever known. She also knows her place in those moments. She is truly driven by being the person God created her to be in every circumstance of life. This is why nothing is too big for her. She simply goes into the situation with a faith that the situation has within it the potential for something good.

Our pastor, Greg Depriest, shared in one of his sermons that the moment we are saved, God sees us the way He will see us forever. In other words, God sees us as the glorious creature He created us to be without the warts, the imperfections, the weaknesses, and those ugly parts that surface in this world. God simply sees us when we allow Him into our lives as the beautiful completed work. It seems Debbie is able to see herself as God sees her. She sees the beauty, the wholeness, and the goodness and not in a prideful way but with a sense of humility that simply affirms what God has done in her life.

Chapter 5

The Difference God Makes:
Because He Lives

In my conversation with Debbie prior to starting the book, I asked her several questions to gain a better understanding about how she viewed her life. Here are a few of the questions:

> What are some of the most important things to focus on in life?

> What helped you deal with the challenges in your life?

> Where did you learn the most important lessons in your life?

> Where did you learn to have such a positive view of life?

Debbie's first response to each of these questions was "God." Knowing Debbie her entire life, it is apparent that God is the center and most important part of her life. Over the years, Mom and I had numerous conversations related to various aspects about Debbie's life. The themes in those conversations were things like: how miraculous her life was; concern about how she might deal with the next physical or situational challenge; and, amazement that she was so positive, joyful, and kind in spite of her limitations. At the end of many of those conversations, I would tell Mom it seemed Debbie had an angel on her shoulder. Regardless of the incredible character of this young woman and the wonderful parents, family, and friends that surrounded her, it was obvious there was something greater at work in her life. The courage, strength, determination, joy, and grace so ever present in her daily living are not of this world. There has to be a greater power at work. Years ago, I stopped worrying about Debbie because of her deep faith in God. It was obvious she was in God's hands, and He was protecting and caring for her in a unique way.

When I say unique, I do not mean that what God does for Debbie is denied the rest of us. In fact, I believe God would love to keep all of us in the safety and security of His hands. However, we typically start feeling our oats, and we jump out of those wonderful hands believing that we can take care of things ourselves. This is when I have gotten into some real messes.

I believe Debbie was taught at an early age that if she would accept Christ and allow God to take residence in her life that He would be her constant source of help. Being so grounded in scripture, Debbie can draw encouragement from Psalm 46:1 where it says: *God is our refuge and strength, A very present help in trouble.*

In that long conversation with Debbie about her life, I asked questions about her challenges and what was important to her. Her responses were so consistent, clear, and certain. Practically everything boiled down to loving God and everyone. When I left that conversation, I called Marcie and she asked me how it went. My response was Debbie makes life sound so simple. Don't we often make life so much more complicated than it really is? When Jesus was asked, in Luke 18:18, "*what shall I do to inherit eternal life?*" the religious scribe was really testing Him. He wanted to expose Jesus as not having a deep understanding of the scriptures. If Jesus had asked that question of the scribe, his response would have been a lengthy discourse on the Torah and the importance of obeying the hundreds of laws recorded there. Jesus' response was short and simple and also reflected an understanding of the Torah that was much deeper than the scribe. Jesus pulled his response from two passages, Deuteronomy 6: 4-5 and Leviticus 19:18. Christ's response recorded in Luke 10:27 was: *Thou shalt love the Lord thy God with all thy heart, and with all thy soul, and with all thy strength, and with all thy mind; and thy neighbor as thyself.*

This response indicates the secret to eternal life is not about our goodness but our love for God and others. Jesus helped us see more about the type of life he offers us in John 10:10. This verse says: *The thief cometh not, but that he may steal, and kill, and destroy: I came that they may have life, and may have it abundantly.* Jesus was not just offering us something for the future but a life of abundance today.

So simple. Debbie did not allow the accident to rob, kill, or destroy the possibilities of a meaningful life. This is what Debbie was saying in all her responses. Debbie gets it. Her simple focus on loving God and those around her provides her abundant joy each and every day. This is why it seems there is an angel on her shoulder. God's presence is so real to her every moment because she is seeking to love God and others each moment. By doing this, Debbie can be positive with negative things happening around her. Debbie can smile when most of us would be crying. Debbie can find joy in the midst of pain. Debbie can find contentment in the little things of life. She can be happy with few material goods.

Those around Debbie see this. Her father said she taught him to love more deeply. Her friends at Woods say that she keeps them going. When people leave a visit with her, they feel better. Debbie told me that she wants people to like her. This is not about her, because when you are with her the focus of the conversation is always about you, not her. I believe she loves others so much she hopes others see her the same way.

Knowing Debbie's love for gospel music, I asked her once what her favorite songs were. The first one she mentioned was "Because He Lives." My father also loved this song and I can still remember him leading it in our church when I was growing up. It is no wonder this is Debbie's favorite song. It is about love, healing, grace, assurance, and victory. God's love radiates through Debbie. God's healing hand gave her abundant life when it seemed the accident would deny her of a meaningful life. God assures her of an ultimate victory which provides assurance her mom can walk and see now that she is with our heavenly Father. The beautiful chorus of this song helps us understand why Debbie does not live in fear. Above all, those words explain why life is worth the living for Debbie despite the pain, the limitations, and the adversities of life.

"Because He Lives" is one of the many great songs written by Bill and Gloria Gaither. It is interesting to know the circumstance that inspired them to write this song. They were expecting a child and were experiencing some difficulties in their lives. As Gloria reflected on bringing a child into a world that is not always wonderful, she experienced a lot of anxiety and sadness. Gloria and Bill drew tremendous hope and strength from their faith which inspired the words to "Because He Lives." I'm sure the words to this wonderful song have inspired many like Debbie who have faced tremendous life challenges.

My favorite hymn is "Turn Your Eyes Upon Jesus" by Helen H. Lemmel. Every time I hear or simply reflect on the words of that song, tears come to my eyes because of the overwhelming love I experience when I think about seeing Jesus face to face. Debbie's eyes are so focused on Jesus and the life she has in Christ. This results in the adversity she has experienced on this earth growing strangely dim.

The constant presence of God is evident in Debbie's life in a manner seldom seen. Two of my favorite passages of scripture describe very well why this Godly presence is so apparent in Debbie.

The first passage is from Paul's letter to the church at Corinth. Paul was trying to get them to focus on the essentials of our faith and he brings it back to loving God and others just as Debbie does. In 1 Corinthians 13: 4-8 Paul says:

4 Love suffereth long, and is kind; love envieth not; love vaunteth not itself, is not puffed up,

5 doth not behave itself unseemly, seeketh not its own, is not provoked, taketh not account of evil;

6 rejoiceth not in unrighteousness, but rejoiceth with the truth;

7 beareth all things, believeth all things, hopeth all things, endureth all things.

8 Love never faileth: but whether there be prophecies, they shall be done away; whether there be tongues, they shall cease; whether there be knowledge, it shall be done away.

In Galatians 5:22-23, Paul shares with the Christian communities in the province of Galatia what our lives will look like if God's Spirit is allowed to lead us.

22 But the fruit of the Spirit is love, joy, peace, longsuffering, kindness, goodness, faithfulness,

23 meekness, self-control; against such there is no law.

An examination of these characteristics of love and a life led by God's Spirit reveals to me that Debbie possesses them as much as anyone I've ever known. Here are some of the examples of these traits:

> Kind: She greets everyone with a smile and shows an interest in the lives of the people she encounters.

> Joyful: She celebrates the good things in your others' lives and is not envious.

> Humble: She never brings attention to things she's accomplished.

> Respectful: She always treats people as if they have worth and value.

> Selfless: She is always mindful of and sensitive to the wants and needs of others.

> Patient: She does not make demands upon others.

> Graceful: She truly forgives others who make mistakes or fail to keep their commitments.

> Protective: Protecting others is very important to Debbie. She has protected her family at times from worrying about the pain or discomfort she is experiencing.

Hopeful: She always finds the positive and good in things.

Trusting: She shows such complete trust in God and those who care for her and all she needs.

Steadfast: She has shown this in spades as she has dealt with so many physical and other setbacks.

Peaceful: She finds peace in the turmoil of life including her mother's death.

These spiritual qualities permeate Debbie's life. As her cousin, Kathy, shared, we are all amazed at how she continually demonstrates these positive characteristics in the midst of great adversity. Only by allowing God to work in an extraordinary way could that happen. Debbie has done that.

One of my favorite pop songs is "I Still Haven't Found What I'm Looking For" by U2. The words of the song share the story of spiritual yearning. They describe how we climb, run, crawl, and scale obstacles in search of satisfaction in our lives. This pursuit points out a variety of approaches from touching fingertips to holding the devil's hand. None of these things satisfy and we come to the refrain repeating over and over the frustration of not finding what the singer is looking for. This is such a sad song in many respects but it resonates with all of us because life is very much about the search for meaning and happiness. Finding that place of complete contentment in life is a real challenge, and all of us struggle at times in our search. That's why this song speaks to us.

Several years ago my wife and I attended a Christian music concert. The opening group for the main act sang "I Still Haven't Found What I'm Looking For." However, after the last verse, the group changed the words of the refrain, which is a repetition of the title to the song, to "I now have found what I'm looking for". As I listened to that refrain being repeated over and over, tears came to my eyes because this changed the song from one of sadness and the futility of failed searching to the joy of a yearning that has been fulfilled. As a Christian, this reminds me of my failed searches and the incredible joy associated with finding and knowing God through my relationship with Christ. When we focus on our Savior and Lord, we can experience life, faith, hope, and love every moment in our lives. Debbie has helped me believe with greater certainty this is really possible no matter what happens. So I can respond with Debbie, "I'm fine."

RICK TOOMEY

Epilogue

Meaning of Debbie's Life to Me

I've tried to tell Debbie's story objectively and without bias, which is difficult because I believe she is an incredible person and she is a cousin I love dearly. My hope is Debbie's story will be a source of encouragement to anyone facing adversity. Her life is a dramatic example of how God's grace is sufficient in any situation life presents us.

This chapter will draw significantly from Debbie's life but will have a different focus. I want to share my personal reflections on the significance of Debbie's life beyond dealing with adversity. When I really examine Debbie's life, I'm compelled to address the question, "so what?" In light of what I see going on in our world, what can I learn from this life being lived so well? Debbie has discovered an approach to life that is not just about overcoming adversity. It is about living a loving, joyful, and meaningful life. Unfortunately this is not the quality of life that many people and even many Christians have today.

After much reflection, I believe Debbie's life has this wonderful quality because of the set of Christian values she uses to guide her life. As I began to identify those values, it seemed they stand in stark contrast to some of the values that are so prevalent in our world and even among many Christians and churches. I believe the values that seem to guide many in the Christian community produce discord, a lack of joy, and a diminished positive influence in our world. I believe we, as Christians and the body of Christ, can all learn a lot from Debbie about the way God wants us to live in this world. In John 10: 10, Jesus said: *"I am come that they might have life, and that they might have it more abundantly."* I believe Debbie has found a few of the keys to that type of abundant life. That's what I want to share.

In sharing what I believe are keys to the abundance of Debbie's life, I will contrast them with worldly values that seem too prevalent in our Christian community.

In sharing these thoughts, I must emphasize two points. First of all, in 1 Corinthians 13: 12, Paul writes to the church at Corinth: *For now we see in a mirror, darkly; but then face to face: now I know in part; but then shall I know fully even as also I was fully known.* What Paul said to the Christians in Corinth applies to all of us today and certainly to me. I know that my viewpoint on the influence of Christianity today is not totally accurate and someday when I sit at the feet of my Father I will see it as it was. The ideas in this chapter are just my thoughts on what I see in Debbie's life compared to much of the Christian community today. There seems to be a major difference, and Debbie's actions seem to be more like what I believe Christ is calling us to do.

Secondly, my thoughts are not intended to be a judgment on any Christians or churches. In fact, I will address this issue of being judgmental later. I believe that the vast majority of Christians are truly seeking to follow Christ and live their lives accordingly. However, we all fall short and we must be willing to examine our lives together in love and without judgment. To me, that means we're willing to acknowledge our sins, our failures, and our shortcomings without condemning one another. Hopefully, these thoughts will not have a judgmental tone.

These thoughts will be shared in the context of choices I believe Debbie has made in her life and choices we must make each day. It has become obvious to me that Debbie's choices are guided by a set of Christian values, principles, and view of life.

In reflecting on this, the work of Viktor Frankl came to mind. I read Frankl's best selling book, Man's Search for Meaning, in 1974, and it is one of those few books that profoundly affected my views about life. Frankl was a Jewish psychiatrist from Austria. The book describes his experiences in Nazi concentration camps. For sixth months Frankl endured painful and dehumanizing experiences at the hands of his German captors. During that same time his mother, wife and brother were killed in some of those same camps. His earlier work on the psychology of philosophical thinking became critical to his survival in those concentration camps. He began to observe that there were two types of prisoners in those camps which he described as either decent people or un-principled ones. The un-principled ones responded to their German captors with hate and deep resentment. The decent prisoners responded with love and kindness in spite of the way they were being treated. Frankl also observed that these "decent" prisoners seemed to thrive despite the terrible conditions. The un-principled ones struggled and died sooner. This ability to love despite how you are being treated is what he described as the ultimate freedom. That freedom is our ability to choose how we respond to the circumstances in our lives. The quote I have always remembered from the book is: "Forces beyond your control can take away everything you possess except one thing, your freedom to choose how you will respond to the situation." Frankl had his liberty, his health, most of his family, and his wealth taken away, but his response was to affirm love for others and find meaning in his suffering. This enabled him to write this great book and teach at great educational institutions like Harvard and lecture all over the world on the importance of a principle-driven life.

The original German title for Man's Search for Meaning was Saying Yes to Life in Spite of Everything: A Psychologist Experiences the Concentration Camp. Discovering the original title brought a smile to my face because "saying yes to life" describes Debbie's response to life so beautifully. She uses the freedom to choose her response to terrible adversity by saying yes to life. This positive response to every circumstance combined with God's working in her life has resulted in a life full of meaning beyond anything we could have imagined.

The following viewpoints are the ones that I believe have guided Debbie's choices throughout her life. These are also viewpoints which represent fundamental Christian values. I believe God desires that we use these values to guide our decisions and actions. I also believe an examination of the life of Jesus will reveal that these same values are reflected in his teachings and the choices He made. Please consider these choices.

Choosing to Focus More on Loving Than Being Good

The first contrast I would like to examine relates to the guiding focus in our lives. Debbie consistently communicates what is important in life and what provides her guidance. It is always about loving God and everyone. Debbie has a singular focus. She is not distracted by lesser things. She doesn't get caught up in what others do, the do's and don'ts, the letter of the law, or a religious code. Jesus did not fall into that trap when asked about the greatest law. Debbie has avoided that trap as well. She keeps her focus on what will demonstrate love for God and others.

As cited earlier, in Mark 12: 30-31, Jesus boiled the commandments down to: *And you shall love the Lord thy God with all thy heart, and with all thy soul, and with all thy mind, and with all thy strength. The second is this; You shall love your neighbor as yourself. There is none other commandment greater than these.*

It is easy to say "Yes, I love God in this way and my neighbor as myself." However, how do the thoughts we express, the decisions we make, and the actions we take in dealing with the circumstances and people we encounter each day provide evidence to what we say?

When I try to put myself in the shoes of non-Christians, I must conclude that most Christians and the church in general are not seen as the beacon of love in our world. In saying this, I at the same time must acknowledge there are millions of Christians who do demonstrate this type of love on a daily basis. I also recognize there are many churches doing wonderful loving things. For many people, a Christian or a Christian church has been instrumental in pointing them to Christ which led to their lives being transformed in a positive way.

What I am trying to say is that I believe most people in the world do not see Christians or the church of Jesus Christ as the shining light of love in this world. Drawing that conclusion saddens my heart because sharing the love of Christ is the most important thing in the world to me and I'm a part of the Christian community that I believe is failing in this respect.

Debbie is seen as a shining light of love in her world. To all who know her, Debbie makes them feel loved and special. It is important to note that it was not primarily Debbie's words but her actions that have consistently created that impression.

So in answering the "So what?" question, I want to reflect on the way Debbie goes about demonstrating that love in contrast to the way Christians and the church often seek to demonstrate God's love.

The book that influenced my early thinking about how to demonstrate my love to God and others was In His Steps by Charles Sheldon. In this book, we see a church and a minister going through the motions of living their Christian faith until the pastor in the story, Henry Maxwell, has an encounter with a tramp, who is out of work and near death. The man knocks on Rev. Maxwell's door and asks for help. The stodgy minister is more concerned with preparing a good sermon for Sunday than helping the man. He sends him away with good wishes. A few days later, the tramp comes into First Church and interrupts Maxwell's well prepared sermon with some piercing words. This man in need confronts the pastor and his congregation about how they were more focused on playing religion than living out their faith in a troubled world. During the week that followed, Rev. Maxwell cannot escape the words of the dying man. That next Sunday, Maxwell delivers a sermon which transformed the thinking of many in his congregation about "the definition of Christian discipleship." He challenges a wealthy and traditional congregation to live for one year constantly being guided by the question, "What would Jesus do?" In addition he wanted them to respond honestly in their actions without counting the cost.

Knowing what Christ would do or say in every circumstance of life is not easy. Our pastor preached one of the greatest sermons I've ever heard a few months ago that captured a perspective which I believe is critical to being able to demonstrate the type of love Christ had. Greg shared that in the Garden of Eden, the options we have to respond to life's circumstances are captured in the tree of the knowledge of good and evil. Human beings now have the option of responding to the events of our life in a good or evil manner. Sin came into the world as Adam partook of the forbidden fruit of the tree of the knowledge of good and evil, and we have been sinning ever since. Thankfully, through Christ we can be forgiven and through the guidance and power of God's Spirit, we can live a life dominated by good and not evil. The irony Greg shared in the sermon, which I believe to be true, is that what got Adam and Eve in trouble was focusing on this tree. They took their eyes off of God and focused on the knowledge of good and evil. If we focus on being good and not being bad, we will never succeed. Paul understood this when he said in Romans 7:15: *For that which I do I know not: for not what I would, that do I practice; but what I hate, that I do.* Isaiah 64:6 says: *all our righteousness are as a polluted garment.* This suggests that my efforts to be righteous are futile and not likely to be productive. I will either fail and feel constant shame and guilt or I will do some good things in the sight of others and become prideful and arrogant which is sinful. We need to be more concerned about expressing God's love and less about establishing our merit as Christians.

Greg indicated that instead of keeping our eyes on being good and not bad, we need to focus our attention upon God. When we focus on God, He leads us, and we end up being more likely to make the choices He desires for us. And when we don't, we will quickly see it and experience His grace as we get back on course. When we focus on God, one aspect of God should stand out above all other characteristics. That preeminent trait is love. 1 John 4:8 says: *He that loveth not knoweth not God; for God is love.* When we focus on God, we will see love. If we're focusing on God, the love we see will inspire us to demonstrate that love to those around us. If we don't demonstrate love, even though we think we are doing the right thing, then our acts are of no value. Paul pointed this out to the church at Corinth. When some members were elevating themselves for speaking in tongues, which they believed was the righteous thing to do, Paul said in 1 Cor. 13:1: *If I speak with the tongues of men and of angels, but have not love, I am become sounding brass, or a clanging cymbal.* In other words even doing the right thing is worthless unless it is done in love.

From my perspective, one of the most dramatic and sad examples of focusing on good and evil and not God's love is the actions of Westboro Baptist Church. This church came to prominence in 1998 for picketing the funeral of a young man by the name of Matthew Shepard in Laramie, Wyoming. Matthew was allegedly beaten to death by two men because he was a homosexual. The congregation were trying to make a statement about their belief that homosexuality is a sin that God hates and is greater than other sins. Regardless of how God might see homosexuality or any other sin, we should always look to the example of Christ as to how we are to respond to the sin of others. Be it a young man who is homosexual or any person whose behavior is different from our moral compass, there is no basis for taking that life. Christ associated with adulterers, liars, thieves, cheats, and murderers. He always reached out to them in love and with respect. To use a funeral to make a statement about what I believe about a sin is not Christ-like. I believe Jesus would embrace the loved ones of Matthew Shepard and express His sadness for their loss.

Numerous major church denominations have denounced the activities of Westboro Baptist Church. However, probably the most Christ-like response to the misguided efforts of Westboro Baptist is the response of two students at Oregon State University. Westboro announced the intention to picket and demonstrate at a service to honor Army Ranger Cody James Patterson. Ranger Patterson lost his life to save others when he embarked on a mission to stop a suicide bomber in Afghanistan. The mission stopped the bombing but Ranger Patterson and three other soldiers died carrying out the mission. In spite of his heroism, Westboro wanted to demonstrate based on their belief that Ranger Patterson and other soldiers had died because God's wrath was bringing punishment due to the homosexual and other sins of America. When the two students, Matt Enloe and Lexie Lynn Merrill, heard about Westboro's plans to picket the memorial service, they organized a Facebook event to mobilize a peaceful counter protest. The community responded and 2,500 people showed up and Westboro cancelled its demonstration. What a beautiful expression of love and respect! I believe this is what Jesus would do.

Actions like those of these two students communicate love - that is our primary responsibility as Christians. The love Christ expressed by giving his life on the cross has transformed our world and the lives of millions of people. As Christians, if we could more consistently respond in love to events and our life experiences each day, I believe people would be drawn to Christ and, as a result, good would be more prevalent in our world.

This is what I observe with Debbie. She is not focused on being good, even though she is a very good person. Her focus in life is loving God and everybody and her actions reflect that. She inspires me to do the same. Debbie is a tremendous ambassador for Christ, not because of her goodness but because of her love.

Choosing Acceptance/Inclusion
Instead of Judgment/Exclusion

My seminary experience enabled me to hear some incredible speakers and sit at the feet of some tremendous teachers. One of the people who impacted me most was a chapel speaker we had by the name of John Howard Griffin. He came out on stage and sat in a chair as he spoke. He also wore a beard. The beard and necessity of sitting was the result of bone deterioration throughout his body caused by drugs and treatments he had taken to change the color of his skin to look like a black person. He did this because he wanted to explore the plight of African-Americans in the south and believed the only way he could do that was to look like a black person.

In 1959, after going through treatments to darken his skin, he traveled for weeks in New Orleans and Mississippi with brief trips to South Carolina and Georgia. He then wrote about those experiences in the book, Black Like Me. Even though I had read the book, the impact of his description of those experiences was alarming and sad. He had diabetes, and he described how difficult it was for him to get a drink of water to quench his thirst. He was not allowed to drink from "white" fountains. He would have to walk several extra blocks to get a drink or use the restroom because he appeared to be black. He talked about the hatred he encountered by white people just during the normal course of a day - whether it was a sales clerk, bus driver, or person on the street. The sad part is that many of those people sat in church pews the Sunday before they encountered Mr. Griffin.

He did share that many white people treated him with kindness but they were the minority. He told us that during those weeks he felt "distinctly other than human." Nothing had changed about this man other than the color of his skin. He dressed the same way. He treated others the same way. He was still a Christian with the same values and basic beliefs. But because he appeared to be black, he was treated as if he were less than human.

The saddest story he told about being treated as "distinctly other" occurred when he returned home at the end of his travels. Dressed in the same clothes he always wore, possessing the same Christian values and beliefs, and being basically the same person with the exception of having skin that was slightly darker, he went to worship at his home church. A man he knew greeted him at the door and did not recognize him. This man told him he might be more comfortable worshiping at the black church close by of the same denomination. What a tragic illustration of judgment and exclusion.

Unfortunately, many evangelical Christian denominations were strangely silent on the issue of slavery and then segregation. I believe God was saddened by this. In Galatians 3: 28, Paul stated with great clarity the way God sees every human being: *There can be neither Jew nor Greek, there can be neither bond nor free, there can be no male and female; for ye all are one man in Christ Jesus.* Jesus never treated a person different whether he or she was Jew, Samaritan, or Gentile. Nor did he discriminate based on gender or even a person's moral standing.

This type of acceptance and inclusion of one another is something Jesus addressed directly when He said: *Verily I say unto you, Inasmuch as ye did it unto one of these my brethren, even these least, ye did it unto me* (Matthew 25:40). Jesus is saying when we accept, include and help the ones who are seen as the least among us, then we are accepting, including and helping Him.

The type of acceptance and inclusiveness that I believe God wants us to demonstrate was illustrated by another speaker at seminary. I can not recall his name, but he was a Baptist pastor of an influential church in Little Rock, Arkansas during the turbulent days of integration beginning in 1957 and continuing through the 60s. He supported integration and led his Baptist church to take a position of support. This was not a political statement but a moral statement about our treatment of one another. Because of the stand he took, about half of his congregation left. The pastor said that it was the best thing that ever happened in that church. The church became a shining light of acceptance and inclusion. The church began to grow and became bigger than it was before.

Other Arkansas Baptists played a unifying role in the Little Rock desegregation crisis in 1957. Several ministers signed a petition protesting the efforts of Governor Orval Faubus to prevent integration of Central High School in Little Rock. I believe God smiled because I believe Jesus would have supported integration and equal opportunities for all people. We must be leaders in treating everyone as a child of God and "not distinctly other."

Debbie has never treated anyone different based on the color of their skin or anything that is different about them. Debbie says the desire of her heart is to love everyone.

Another aspect of acceptance is the lack of acceptance we demonstrate due to being judgmental of others based on their beliefs or behavior. Jesus made it very clear through His words and actions that being judgmental is not desirable for a Christian. His clearest statement on this was in Luke 6:37: *And judge not, and ye shall not be judged: and condemn not, and ye shall not be condemned: release, and ye shall be released.*

Making judgments is an inherent part of our personality. The Myers-Briggs Type Indicator (MBTI) is a personality assessment to help identify the natural preferences we have as human beings. There are four paired preferences and one of those is the preference which addresses our general approach to life. We use both of these preferences but we all tend to use one more than the other. One preference is Perceiving which means that even though we all spend a good portion of each day perceiving the world around us, some people go through life paying more attention to observing the world and learning more about it. People who have a preference for Perceiving tend to be curious, adaptable and spontaneous in their approach to life. About 35% of the population lives this way. The majority, about

65%, of the population have the preference of Judging. Even though we all spend part of our day drawing conclusions about and organizing the things we observe around us, people with a preference for Judging approach life in a manner where making judgments about the things they experience is their major focus. They live a life that is organized, decisive, and focused on completing tasks.

This means that we all gather information each day and draw conclusions about that information. About two thirds of the people in the world give most of their energy to making judgments. This does not mean they are judgmental in the way Jesus is describing. Every day we have to make judgments about what to do, when to eat, how to solve a problem, how to do our job, how to discipline a child, etc. Making decisions about what is best for us to do in our lives is an important dimension of our lives. This use of judgment is healthy, necessary, and productive.

The judging that Jesus is warning against is the judgment and condemnation of another person. I believe Jesus modeled best what He meant about not judging and condemning in His encounter with the adulterous woman who was about to be stoned as recorded in John 8:1-11. Here we see Jesus in the temple courts teaching the people who were drawn to Him. The Pharisees, who were religious leaders, brought a woman caught in adultery to Jesus. In an attempt to test and trap Jesus, they asked Him what they should do with the woman. They went on to say that in the Law Moses commanded that a woman caught in adultery should be stoned. Here we see a common response of religious people wanting to use a legalistic approach to address sin. Jesus simply paused and wrote on the ground. Then He straightened up and I'm sure He looked them in the eye, and said, *"He that is without sin among you, let him first cast a stone at her."* Slowly they all, from the oldest and wisest to the youngest and most impulsive, walked away until Jesus was left alone with the woman. He looked at the woman and asked her where her accusers were and whether anyone was now condemning her. She responded that there was no one there to condemn her. Here is where this incredible story goes to another level. No one stayed to condemn this woman because they were not without sin. Now the woman is left with Jesus who was without sin. In spite of His purity, Jesus then said, *" Neither do I condemn thee: go thy way; from henceforth sin no more."* Jesus told us not to condemn others, and He did not. He accepted and affirmed her. Yes, He then encouraged her to leave her life of sin because He loved her and He knew her current lifestyle would not bring fulfillment or joy. I would bet this woman followed Jesus. This is the reason God wants us to accept others and not condemn them. It works.

Years ago, I had the opportunity to apply Jesus' teachings in this area, as a counselor. A lady, who had come to me for assistance with an alcohol problem some years earlier, came to see me about another problem. She had become involved in an affair with a married man. She told me about the situation, and we scheduled another appointment to talk more. As she walked to the door, she turned to me and said, "Weren't you a minister in the past?" I said, "Yes." She then said, "Why didn't you tell me that what I'm doing is wrong?" I asked her if others had told her that. She responded, "Yes." I then asked her if other people telling her that what she was doing was wrong had caused her to get out of the relationship. She said, "No." I also asked her if she believed what she was doing was wrong. She said, "Yes." I then told her, "I'm more interested in helping you make the decision that is best for you. I won't be taking the splinter out of your eye when I have a beam in my own." We talked several more times, and she stopped the affair but not because anyone told her it was wrong. She was a Christian, and I trusted that God's Spirit could do a more effective job of convincing her of the sinfulness of her acts than any person could have.

That is God's job not ours. I believe our responsibility is to accept and not condemn others who are sinners just as we are. Jesus accepted a liar in Peter, a man who led in the persecution of Christians in Paul, a cheat in Zaccheus, the Samaritan woman who was married numerous times, and everyone He encountered. He takes us as we are and works with us. Should we not do the same?

During significant points in my life when I have struggled with sin, I have experienced condemnation from other Christians. Without exception it hurt and was not helpful. The Christians who inspired me to turn away from that sin were the ones who continued to love me and lift me up in their prayers. They neither excused my sinful behavior nor attacked it. They simply cared in a way that helped me do the "right thing." As I took that sin to God, I experienced the acceptance and grace that Jesus consistently gave those He encountered while here with us. The acceptance and grace helped. This is what God wants us to give others.

As I've observed other Christians over the years, the ones who seem the happiest and are the most effective in leading others to a saving relationship with God are the ones who are the greatest instruments of grace and acceptance. They seem to experience an abundance of love, joy, and peace in their lives, and I believe living a life of accepting others and being instruments of grace is the reason their lives are blessed in that way. On the other hand, it seems that the Christians I observe who are constantly condemning and attacking others and their failings are seldom really happy. I believe they are experiencing the condemnation Jesus said we will receive when we condemn others.

It seems to me at times that Christians and churches are more a voice of condemnation than acceptance today. Talk radio hosts who tout themselves to be moral beacons and a lot of Christians on Facebook constantly attack others. There is a hateful and condemning tone in much that is said today. We have people questioning someone's Christianity because of who they vote for in political elections. I have wonderful Christian friends who vote for Republicans and wonderful Christian friends who vote for Democrats. It seems that both parties take positive moral stands on some issues and at times both parties seem to promote policies that do not seem Christ-like. A person's Christianity should not be questioned because of his or her stand on a particular issue. Christians should set the tone for examining issues in a loving way and without condemnation.

Unfortunately, many of our religious leaders and groups lead the way in this type of condemnation. Some examples through the centuries: military campaigns blessed by the Pope in the 11th century against pagans and heretics; Catholic explorers in Mexico executing Aztecs for the practice of human sacrifice; burning of witches at the stake; the Army of God's support of abortion clinic bombings; or, blaming the deaths associated with hurricane Katrina on the lifestyle of a small part of our U.S population.

There are laws that govern society, and the legal systems of society should make appropriate judgments and determine the consequences for violation of those laws. The spiritual judgments for the violation of spiritual laws through our thoughts and actions should remain in God's domain. We will all stand before God and experience that judgment. This spiritual judgment of a person is beyond our wisdom, understanding, and grace. We should leave it in His loving and capable hands.

Condemnation will never change the world or a person. Acceptance and love is what drew people to Christ. We need to follow His words and example. I've never heard Debbie say an unkind word about another person. You don't have to see things the way Debbie does or do things the way Debbie does them. She accepts you as you are.

Members in Alcoholics Anonymous use the expression, "do not take others' personal inventory (personal examination of our moral failings)." This is very good advice because this is exactly what Jesus expects of us. I've always told people that I have a hard enough time taking my own inventory and dealing with the temptations in my life. I don't have time to focus on the inventory of another person. Mine is the only one for which I can seek forgiveness, make amends, and change. If someone asks for my help, I can try to help but not with a spirit of condemnation.

One final thought on Jesus' words in Luke 6:37. He said not to judge and condemn others because you will be judged and condemned in like manner. I am not sure whether Jesus is speaking about the way God or others will judge us. In principle, Jesus is saying that if we judge harshly and often, then we will experience harsh and frequent judgment. I believe if we are accepting of others and gracious toward them, then we will be treated more graciously by God and others.

Choosing Hopefulness/Positivity
Instead of Despair/Negativity

Recall the response that Debbie gave when told about the death of her mother. She paused and said, "Now Mom can see and walk again." Debbie has an abiding faith in God's promise that we will inherit a new body when we go to be with Him. This faith gives her a hope that is real and permeates her life. Remember in 1 Corinthians 13:13 we are told that faith, hope, and love are the three things in life that will abide. In other words these things are really important and they are always there for us, and they have substance and are lasting. Debbie's faith brings her great hope for today and tomorrow and produces a positivity that is infectious.

Our world needs more hope and positivity. We need more people whose glass is half full and not half empty. I've always felt that negativity and cynicism is easy, lazy, and uncaring. If I always look for the worst in everyone and every situation, it is easy because there is probably something wrong with every person and situation. It seems to me that focusing on the negative seldom leads to making things better. Should we approach life with an attitude that does not address real problems? Of course not. But if negativity is our response to life's circumstances, we will be less likely to see possibilities and the positive things that can be used to make things better.

The book, Now Discover Your Strengths by Marcus Buckingham and Donald O. Clifton, presents the concept that we will grow and develop more effectively as human beings if we focus on developing our strengths rather than trying to improve our weaknesses. The authors cite the example that if you send an average reader and an above average reader through a speed reading course, the average reader's speed will increase maybe 60% while the above average reader's speed will increase about 800%. In other words when we focus on the positive strengths in our lives, we get the greatest benefit.

This focusing on the positive is one of the secrets to Debbie's joy and success despite great adversity. As I mentioned earlier, I found the book, The Power of Positive Thinking by Dr. Norman Vincent Peale in some of Debbie's personal items. Dr. Peale's book was quite controversial in the psychological community. Professionals in this field did not believe the book was grounded in sound research and concepts. Dr. Peale was a minister for 52 years and believed that life's problems could be handled with a positive attitude. Many critics believed Dr. Peale's approach did not deal with many of the harsh realities of life. Debbie's positive outlook is not a Pollyanna view that discounts difficulties and challenges. Goodness knows Debbie had to stare almost every day of her life at challenges and limitations that few of us will ever face. It was not a belief in the power that positive thinking in and of itself would enable her to accomplish great things. It was a deeper and abiding faith expressed beautifully in Romans 8: 28: *And we know that to them that love God all things work together for good, even to them that are called according to his purpose.* So when Debbie's mother died, she did not focus on the death or loss of interaction with her mother. Instead she focused on the positive joy of knowing that her mother was no longer limited by lack of sight and inability to walk.

Jesus found good in every situation including the cross. He finds the good in every person. The scriptures are numerous about the importance of approaching life with hope and positivity instead of despair and negativity. Let's look at a few key ones:

Psalms 118:24: This is the day which Jehovah hath made; We will rejoice and be glad in it.

Philippians 4:8: Finally, brethren, whatsoever things are true, whatsoever things are honorable, whatsoever things are just, whatsoever things are pure, whatsoever things are lovely, whatsoever things are of good report; if there be any virtue, and if there be any praise, think on these things.

Proverbs 17:22: A cheerful heart is a good medicine; But a broken spirit drieth up the bones.

Philippians 4:6: In nothing be anxious; but in everything by prayer and supplication with thanksgiving let your requests be made known unto God.

Philippians 4:13: I can do all things in him that strengtheneth me.

Jeremiah 29:11: For I know the thoughts that I think toward you, saith Jehovah, thoughts of peace, and not of evil, to give you hope in your latter end.

From the scriptures above, I would conclude the following:

> With God's help, I can find joy in each day. I do not have to be pulled down by the lack of joy around me.

> If I focus on the good and positive things in life, my life will be lived in a good and positive atmosphere. Unfortunately, I know many Christians who get caught up in the negativity of popular people on talk shows and live in anger, fear, and negativity. This is not where God wants our focus to be.

> With God's help I can find joy in practically every experience in life. This is why Debbie is able to remain joyful

despite pain, surgeries, limitations, or death of loved ones. If she can do that with God's help, then so can we.

No circumstance in life should overwhelm me. The way through that circumstance may not be easy but with God's help we can make it through. By believing that God will strengthen me and enable me to deal with every situation life brings me, I can be positive in spite of the negatives of the situation.

As a Christian, God's plans for me involve my welfare and a future filled with hope. Why be negative and live in despair? God has a positive and hopeful future for me. That is the real source of our positive thinking.

When I read what a lot of Christians post on Facebook or what they express on TV or in person, it is often filled with fear and pessimism about what is happening around them. We want to carry guns to restaurants to protect ourselves from something that might endanger us. We become incredibly anxious about health care, the economy, the price of oil, or the next election. Most of the fears that have been raised in the past never materialized. And even if they had, God assures us if we simply abide in His hope, things will be OK. As Christians, we need to be lights of hope. We need to say to a frightened and desperate world that there is hope in Christ.

Debbie could legitimately complain about numerous things every day of her life. But she does not. She focuses on: things that are true, not the lies; things that are honorable, not dishonorable; justice, not injustice; purity instead of impurity; lovely, not ugly things; commendable acts versus condemnable acts; and, excellence, not failure. Unlike the talking heads on radio and television, Debbie looks for things to praise, not to criticize.

God looked for the good in Abraham, Joseph, and David, and Christ saw the good in Peter, Mary Magdalene, and every person He encountered. He healed the sick, befriended the friendless, brought joy to those in despair. Let's be the same instruments for hope by being positive about people, life, and the future.

Choosing to Use Influence Instead of Power

One of the major challenges Jesus faced with His Jewish followers was confronting their desire for Him to be a Messiah who would be an earthly king. Many of His followers wanted Him to lead a revolt and overthrow their Roman rulers. This desire to have power over our lives and the circumstances that impact our happiness and well-being is a major driver for all human beings. If we believe we are being mistreated by those in power, whether it is the government, our employer, or a parent, our response is often one of revolt. We try to gain dominance over that power so we can have control. Jesus clearly communicated to His followers that the Kingdom He came to establish was a spiritual kingdom and not an earthly one. In John 18:36 Jesus said: *My kingdom is not of this world: if my kingdom were of this world, then would my servants fight, that I should not be delivered to the Jews: but now is my kingdom not from hence.* Jesus was totally focused on establishing a spiritual kingdom, not an earthly one. This focus was so razor sharp that Jesus never focused on the ills, injustices, or problems with the Roman Empire. In fact when the Pharisees tried to pull Him into the politics of earthly power by asking Him if it is lawful to give tribute unto Caesar, or not, His response in Matthew 22: 19-21 was: *Show me the tribute money. And they brought unto him a denarius. And he saith unto them, whose is this image and superscription? They say unto him, Caesar's. Then saith he unto them, render therefore unto Caesar the things that are Caesar's; and unto God the things that are God's.*

It seems to me that a large segment of the Christian community gets caught up excessively in the political world today. Beginning with the Moral Majority, Christians have become more and more involved in politics to bring about a change in moral issues. Legislating moral issues is increasingly the focus of many Christians. Use of political power to control the circumstances of life and create the environment that is most in line with our spiritual beliefs is becoming the norm for many Christians. Should we vote our conscious? Absolutely. Some level of political involvement is appropriate. However, much of the activity of Christians in politics today seems similar to the way Jesus' followers tried to make Jesus into an earthly King. When we focus excessively on making government and laws consistent with the moral mandates of our faith, I believe we become more of a hammer of compliance instead of a beacon of light. Nowhere did Jesus try to mandate discipleship. It was always a call to individual commitment. God's Spirit moves in the lives of individuals to make them aware of their sin and the emptiness in their lives. God, through Christ, then offers every human being hope for a life filled with forgiveness and meaning.

The woman at the well, Zachaeus, Nicodemus, and the disciples were ultimately drawn to Christ because of the power of His personal influence in their lives, not a cause or political position to rally around.

In Matthew 5:13-16 Jesus said: *Ye are the salt of the earth: but if the salt have lost its savor, wherewith shall it be salted? it is thenceforth good for nothing, but to be cast out and trodden under foot of men. Ye are the light of the world. A city set on a hill cannot be hid. Neither do men light a lamp, and put it under the bushel, but on the stand; and it shineth unto all that are in the house. Even so let your light shine before men; that they may see your good works, and glorify your Father who is in heaven.*

I believe in many ways the salt of our Christian faith has lost its power. It seems that we are more focused on dictating our beliefs to others and expecting everyone to live by the beliefs we aspire to follow than living out a life of demonstrating the love and transforming power of God in the life of an individual. Salt is a powerful substance. It seasons everything it touches. It is a preservative that prolongs the life of food. For such an unassuming substance, it has great influence. It seems that as Christians, we are trying to overpower the world instead of being the salt of the earth and a beacon on a hill that people can seek out in the darkness.

Another manifestation of the excessive focus on power and control instead of influence is the way some in the Christian community attack various parts of the world around us. We attack Hollywood, anyone who doesn't honor the things we honor, or anyone who expresses a view counter to our Christian faith. What do we expect? We act sometimes as if this is something earlier Christians never faced. The world is no more sinful and hostile toward Christianity today than it has ever been. In fact, we Americans live in the most Christian friendly environment today than at any time in history. For example, as I am writing this morning, a headline on the front page of our local paper reads, "Faith Is Spelled R-I-S-K - Former local couple planning to establish church in Africa." A recent segment called Making A Difference on the NBC evening news highlighted the work of a faith based group in caring for the homeless. I can worship anywhere I want and anytime I want. I can share my faith in the training I do with a local company. I can lift a prayer to God any time I want to, whether it is at work, at school, or in Walmart. Publicly pronounced prayers in certain environments is a limitation and one I support because everyone in most of those situations might not ascribe to that expression to God. I do not want to impose my prayer upon others. Prayer is a very personal thing between me and God. It is not for public display. I'm very comfortable with corporate prayer and I participate in that daily with my family and others who share my beliefs.

I hear Christians today talk about being persecuted because someone takes a view that is different from theirs, attacks their viewpoint, or acts differently from them. The sins of the world around me and others believing and acting different from me are not persecution. When Christians claim they are being persecuted because someone said something bad about them or disagreed with them, I feel like we are being so disrespectful of the early Christians and other Christians through the years who were thrown to the lions, hung on a cross, or gave their lives in other ways. What we experience from the world around us today is nothing in comparison.

Another illustration of how we battle unnecessarily with the world around us is our war on the "war on Christmas." A wonderful Christian gentleman, Jim Welch, who writes articles for our local paper shared some insightful thoughts during the recent Christmas season. Those thoughts closed with:

> "We Christians have failed our faith if the only way we can express ourselves is to bully Christ into Christmas. If the joy we profess to hold in our hearts is expressed in scowls about what others might be saying instead of 'Merry Christmas,' we've lost the war before we show up for the battle. If we think the strength of our eternal faith relies on something as fickle as a law of the moment, we are more than a bit short of the mustard seed and moving mountains, truths our faith teaches. Nobody anywhere on the planet - not just here - deserves to be ever fearful of saying 'Merry Christmas,' and no Christian anywhere needs to be fearful of somebody not saying 'Merry Christmas.' If Jesus taught the world anything, it is that it's not how we legislate that we will be judged. It is by how we loved. Merry Christmas."

There is not a power seeking bone in Debbie's body. Debbie has never sought a position of power. She never supervised others or managed an organization. However, when I visit Debbie at Wood Memorial Nursing Home, it seems to me that she has the greatest influence at that facility. When the lady looked at me during one visit and said, "Debbie keeps us going", she was acknowledging the influence Debbie has. Everyone smiles when asked where Debbie is because she uses her influence to bring joy into their lives. She is a shining light.

I have taught various leadership courses over the last 20 years in numerous organizations. I believe the quality of leadership in business, government, education, health care, and every aspect of our society is one of the primary determinants to success and the quality of our lives. Leadership can lead to terrible things like the crimes Germany committed under Hitler's leadership. Leadership can also produce healing and reconciliation as it did in South Africa under the leadership of Nelson Mandela. When I look at great leaders, one quality I see is humility. Much of the research on effective leadership supports this. This implies that even when someone is entrusted with power, it is critical that it be used humbly with consideration of the views and needs of others.

In 1974, Billy Graham came to Southern Seminary in Louisville, Kentucky when I was a student. I can remember the excitement on campus as we anticipated that chapel service. Some students like me came in with great admiration for Rev. Graham. Some were more skeptical about him and his ministry. When he came out on that platform, everyone in the audience sensed something special about this man. The best way I can express the spirit that emanated from the world-renowned evangelist was one of deep humility. He talked about how he admired our commitment to preparing for the ministry. He also shared how pride and the lure of power had resulted in his being used by some political leaders to promote their own agendas, which was not consistent with Rev. Graham's values. He indicated that this was a reminder to him that his focus should be on preaching the gospel he was called to preach and not getting caught up in politics. He renewed his commitment to be a pastor to presidents and not an advocate for their causes. Rev. Graham refocused his efforts on being an influence for Christ and not being seduced by power. His ministry is certainly a great example of being a powerful influence in the world. We need to learn from his experience.

John Acton articulated a danger of seeking power when he said, "Power tends to corrupt, and absolute power corrupts absolutely." In addition to influence being more powerful than the pursuit of power itself, I agree with John Acton that power has the tendency to corrupt. In the Bible, David is a great example of this. David was described as a man after God's own heart, and yet after he became king, the allure of power made him feel he was entitled to have what he wanted. This resulted in him taking Uriah's wife and putting Uriah in the front lines of battle so he would be killed. "Absolute power can corrupt absolutely." This is why I become concerned when individuals or groups of Christians seek worldly power. I am afraid they will use it in a corrupt way and tarnish the real influence of Christianity.

So whether it is in relation to our role as a leader or our daily walk as a Christian, we need to focus on influence and not power. One of John C. Maxwell's books is entitled <u>The 21 Irrefutable Laws of Leadership.</u> The second law of leadership he describes is "The Law of Influence." In discussing this law, he says that "The true measure of leadership is influence - nothing more, nothing less." In reality if leaders cannot influence people to follow them or inspire them to action, they cannot lead. As Christians, if we want to lead others to Christ or enable positive change in our world, we must be able to influence others. Power will not work.

If we choose to try to influence those around us instead of using power to force compliance with our views, what are the keys to being able to influence others? First of all, we have to accept that the other person may not agree or may choose a different path. This is hard for us, and especially if we care deeply for the other person and believe agreement with our viewpoint is in their best interest. But the path of influence leaves the choice to the other person, and if we study the life of Christ, He did that over and over. Many people followed Him, and many rejected Him.

Secondly, we have to genuinely care for the person we are trying to influence. The old expression "I don't care how much you know unless I know how much you care" applies here. If I'm simply trying to gain control over the other person or get him or her to do what is best for me, I will never have significant influence in that person's life. Martin Luther King did more than any other person to advance the cause of equal treatment of people regardless of the color of their skin. He did this through influence and not power and because of the caring way he made his case. He demonstrated that he cared for and had respect for all people. He articulated this when he said: "There is a final reason I think that Jesus says, 'Love your enemies.' It is this: that love has within it a redemptive power. And there is a power there that eventually transforms individuals." He influenced people because he demonstrated love for all people, not just those for whom he was advocating.

Finally, you have to build trust with others and earn the right to influence them. Unless we are forthright, caring, and consistent in our relationships, we will have no influence. There are times I have chosen not to attempt to influence a situation because I did not feel I had earned that right. One way to earn that right is to demonstrate that I value and see the good in others. Henry Drummond said, "The people who influence you are the people who believe in you." If I want to influence others, they must see that I believe in them and value them as an individual. Tearing them down or trying to control them will not work.

It is easy to argue, whether one is a Christian or not, that the most influential person in history is Jesus Christ. We measure time based on his birth. He is the leader of the most prevalent religion in the world. His moral teachings are admired by people who do not even follow Him. Thousands have died for Him. For those of us who know Him as our Savior and Lord, He has transformed our lives. Jesus inspired that following through influence and not power. He did not rule over an organization of thousands. Rather, he had a motley crew of twelve disciples. He did not have a PAC to raise money for His cause; He depended on the sacrificial gifts of His followers. He did not court the seats of power and control. Instead, he invested his time reaching out to the everyday people. He did not invest millions in advertising to shape an attractive message; He sat down with small groups and people one-on-one and shared with them the good news. He changed the world one person at a time by influencing them. This was the source of His power. Should influence, not power, be the source of our strength?

Conclusion

I have not mentioned my father much in telling this story. Dad was a significant part in Debbie's story like the rest of the family. One of the things he probably shared in common with Debbie more than anyone else was a love for gospel music. As I mentioned earlier he led singing in Baptist churches for about 35 years. He did it very well and with a lot of passion. One of his favorite hymns was "Blessed Assurance." As we sang this wonderful hymn recently at our church, it brought tears because of the blessed assurance expressed in the words of this song. The relevance of the words to Debbie's story is striking. I believe that, in spite of life-changing injuries from a tragic automobile accident and a life filled with limitations and challenges, Debbie, through her relationship with Jesus Christ, has found rest, happiness, and blessings that cannot be achieved through her own efforts. As a result, she is able to spend her time each day praising her Savior all day long. This is the joy that all those around her see. This joy is available to all of us if we spend our days praising our Savior.

Debbie has had a tremendous influence on my life, the rest of her family, and friends. The true test of someone's influence in our lives is whether we change inwardly and outwardly. I believe my life has been more loving, more hopeful, more accepting and more focused on influencing those around me in positive ways as a result of having known Debbie. I hope the story of her life and what it means to me will bring about some positive things in the lives of my readers. Whether you are facing adversities, big or small, my desire is that you find hope. If you struggle finding all the joy that life can provide you, my wish is you can see that by changing our attitudes and actions each day we can discover greater joy in life. Finally, if you are looking for direction in your life, I pray you can discover how loving God and others can provide meaning in a way nothing else can. Maybe then we can all sincerely respond when asked how we are with "I'm fine."

ABOUT THE AUTHOR

If the author is asked to describe himself, the first word that comes to mind is blessed. He is blessed to know and serve a God who is gracious and loving.

He is blessed with a wife who is loving and kind and inspires him to be a better person each day. He is blessed with a daughter and son who are wonderful young adults and are a source of great pride. He is blessed with two grandchildren who bring him great joy. He is also blessed with a wonderful family and group of friends, many of whom you will meet in the pages of this book.

His life work is very important to him. Preparing for the variety of professional roles he has played led him to complete a Bachelors of Science in Industrial Management, a Masters in Religious Education, and a Doctorate of Education in Educational and Counseling Psychology.

Service is the focus of his life work and he has served as minister, counselor, trainer, professor, and consultant with great organizations. In addition, he has also served churches as a teacher and elder and his community by providing assistance to numerous non-profit organizations and conducting over 40 community leadership retreats. He has also been blessed to meet people from all over the world as he has done training and consulting in 18 countries.

He is inspired by people and groups doing great things and this is what led him to write this book about an incredible person.

www.ingramcontent.com/pod-product-compliance
Lightning Source LLC
Chambersburg PA
CBHW031622040426
42452CB00007B/637